A work of art that does not begin in emotion is not art.

PAUL CEZANNE

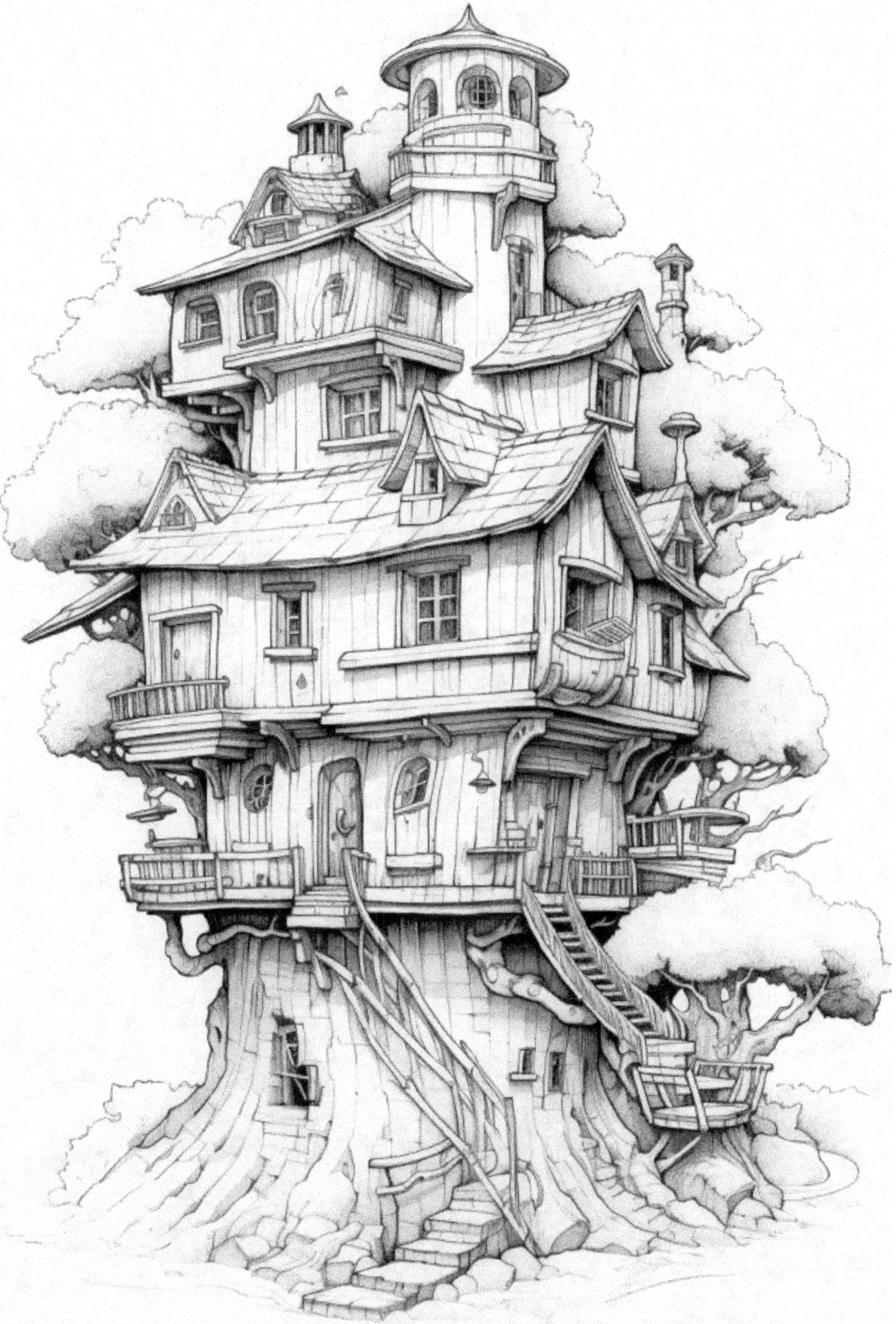

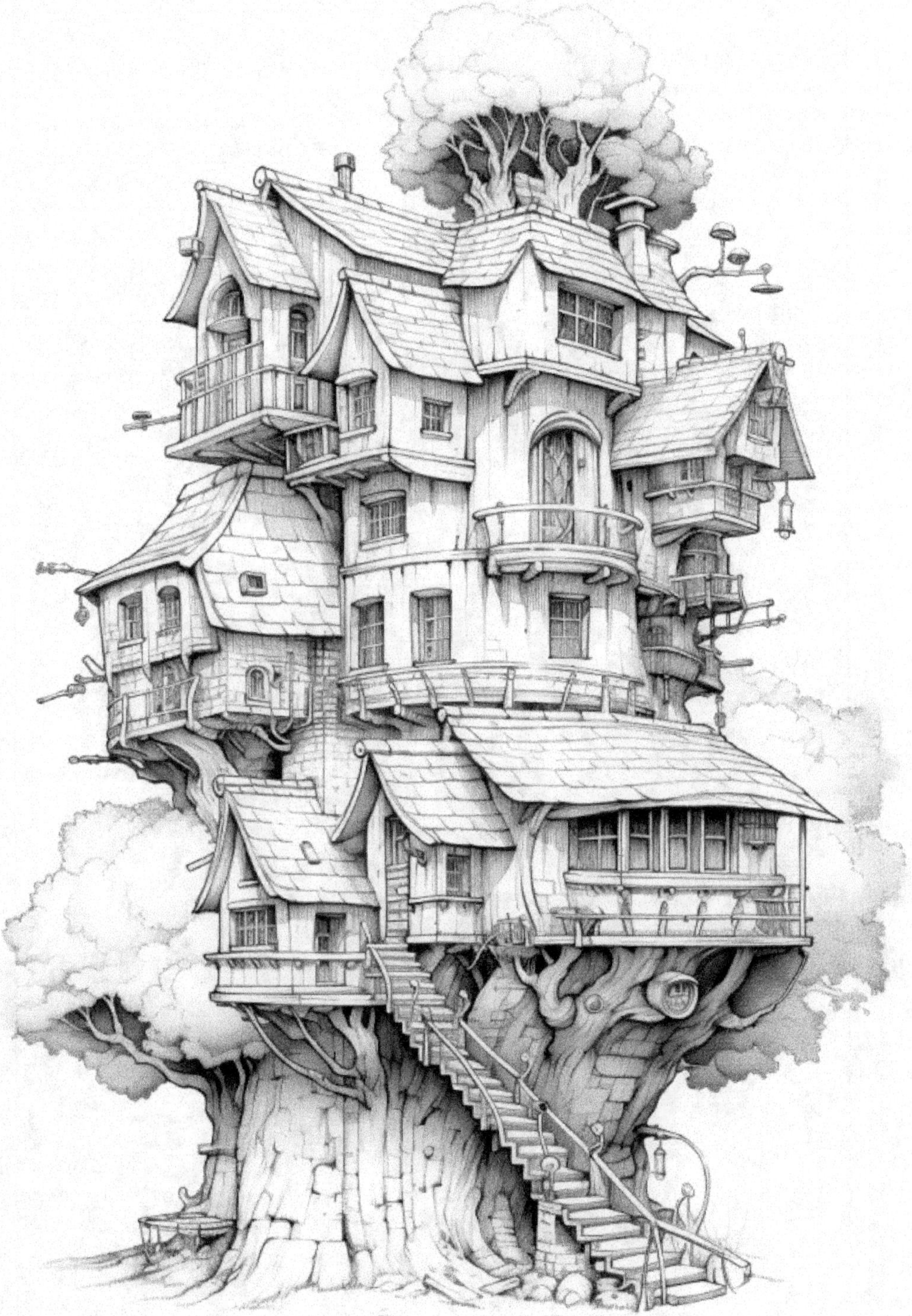

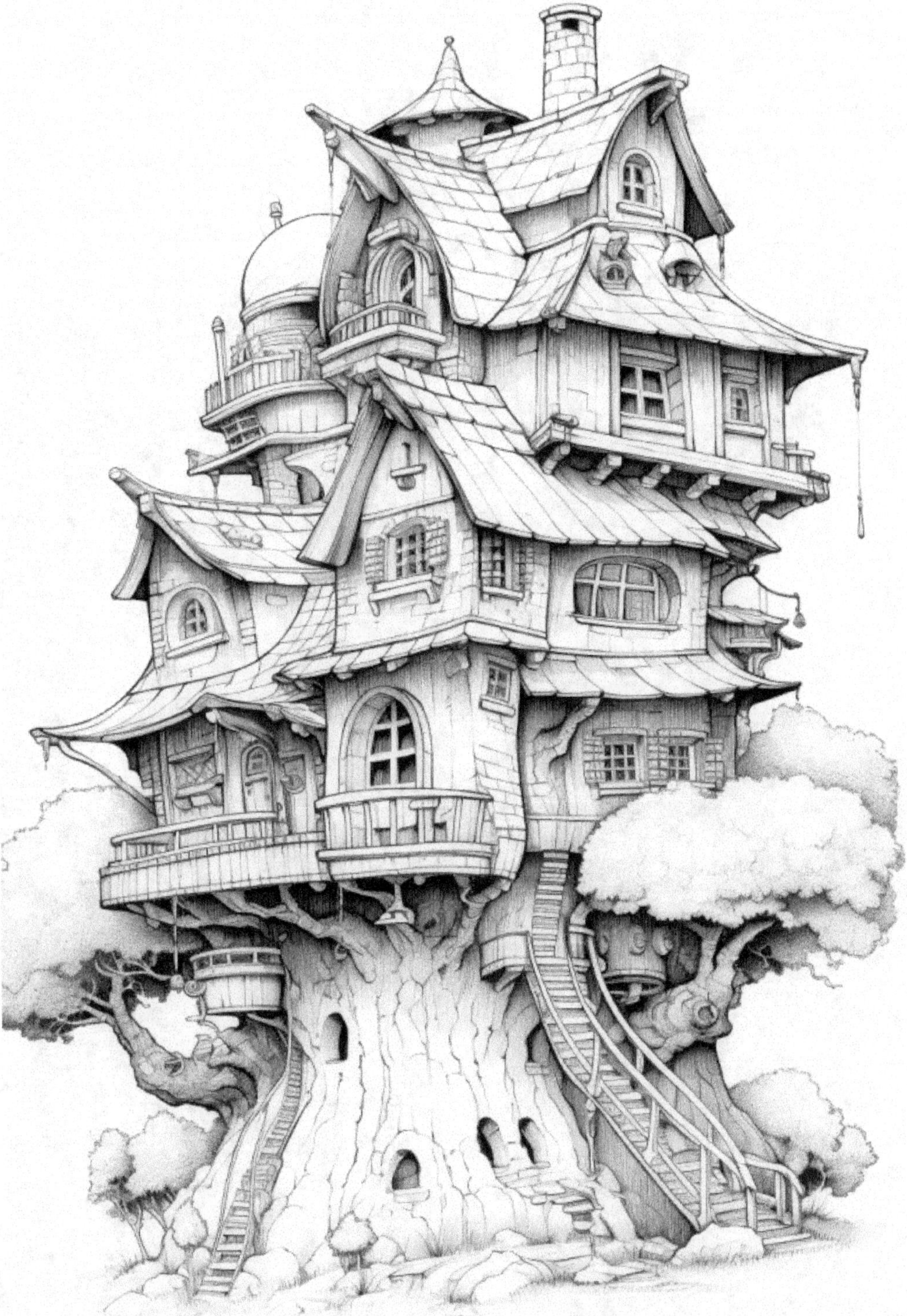

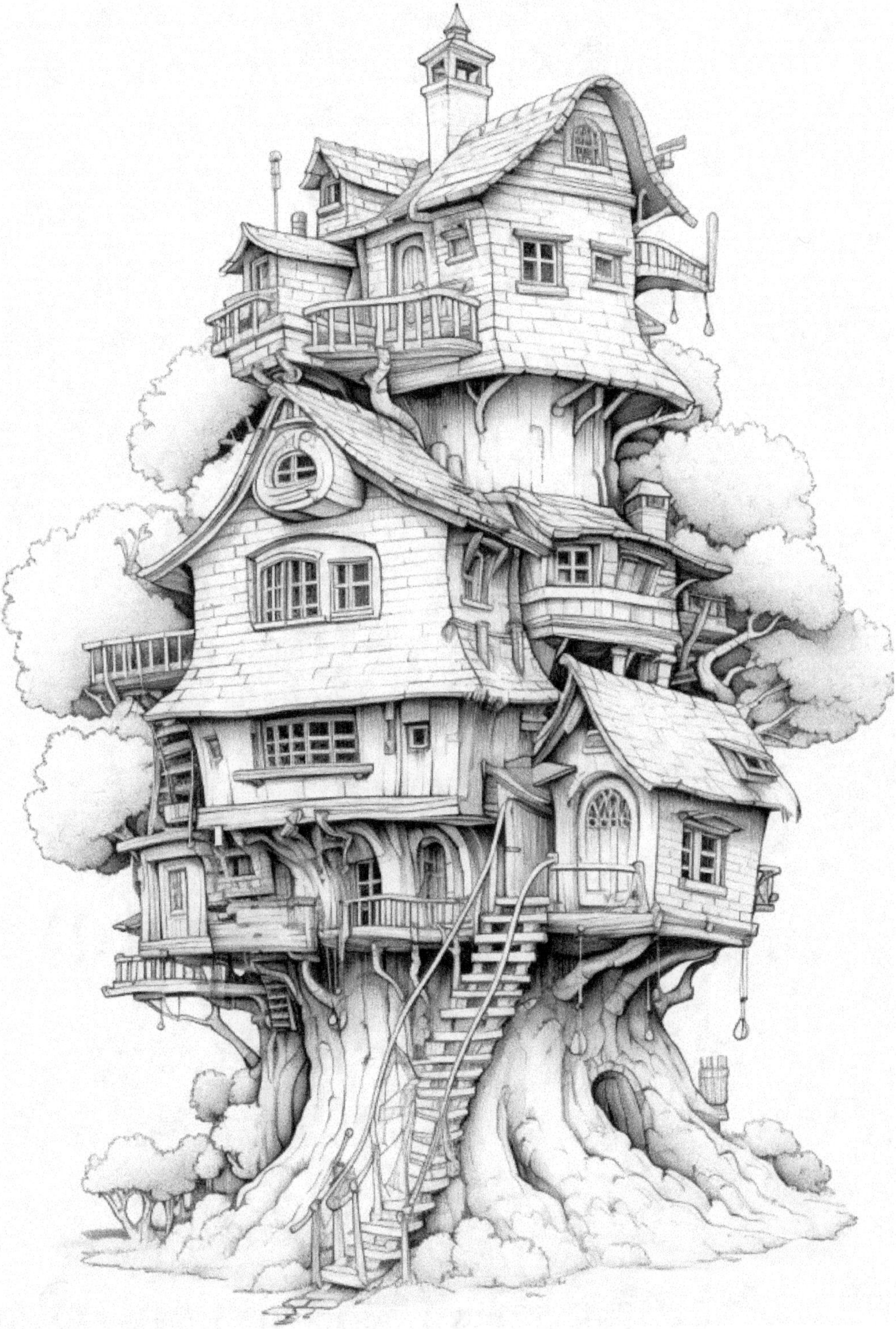

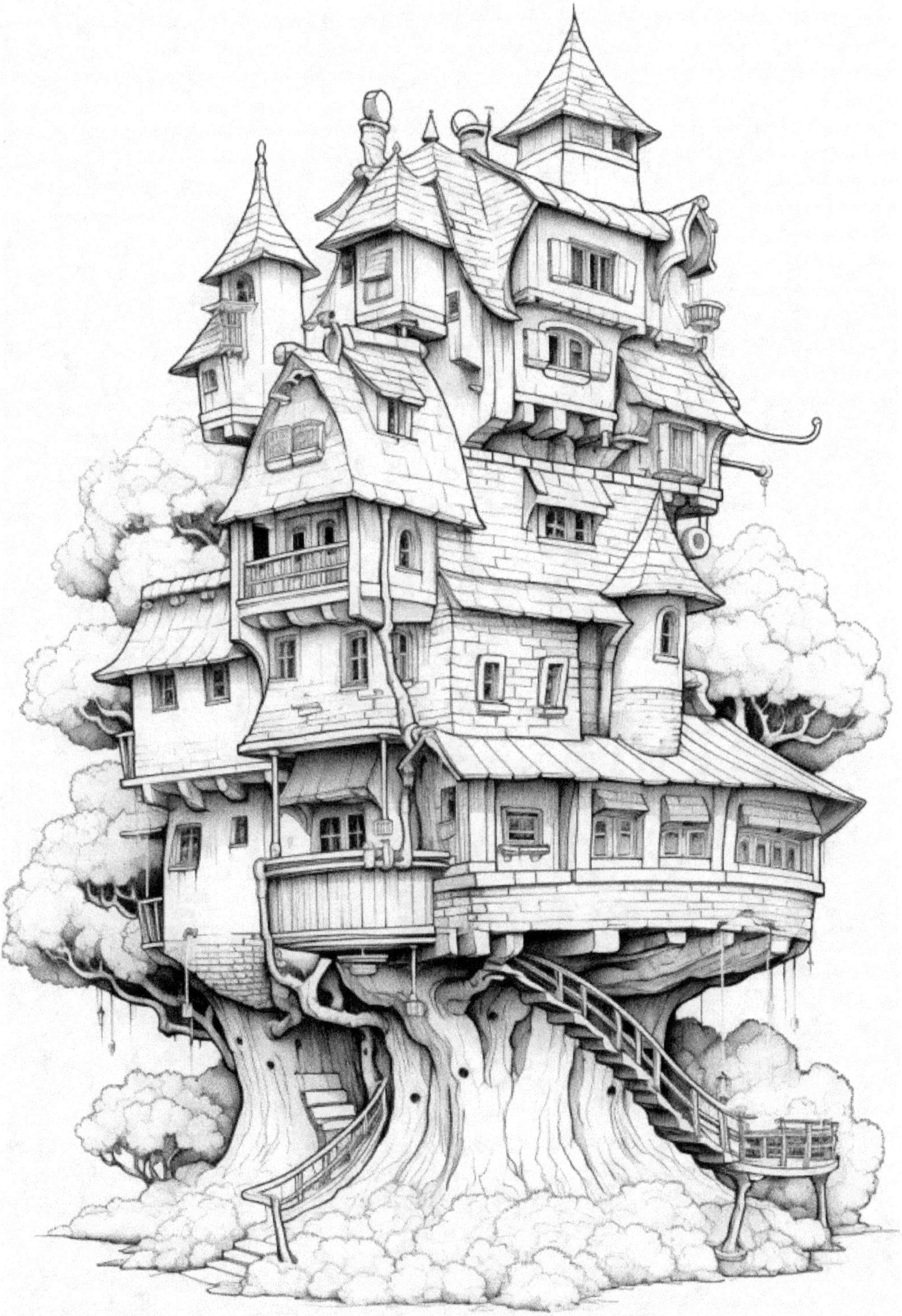

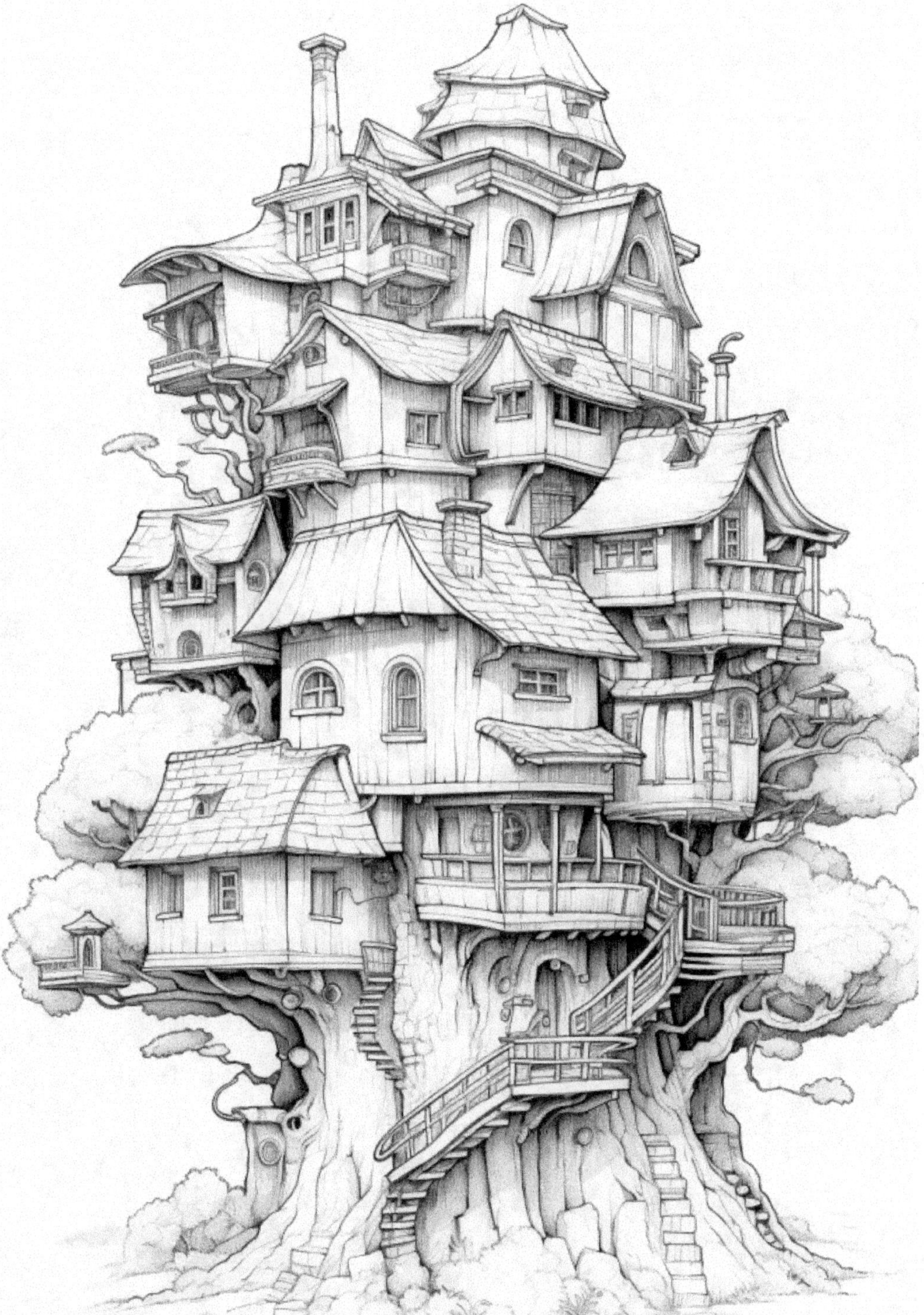

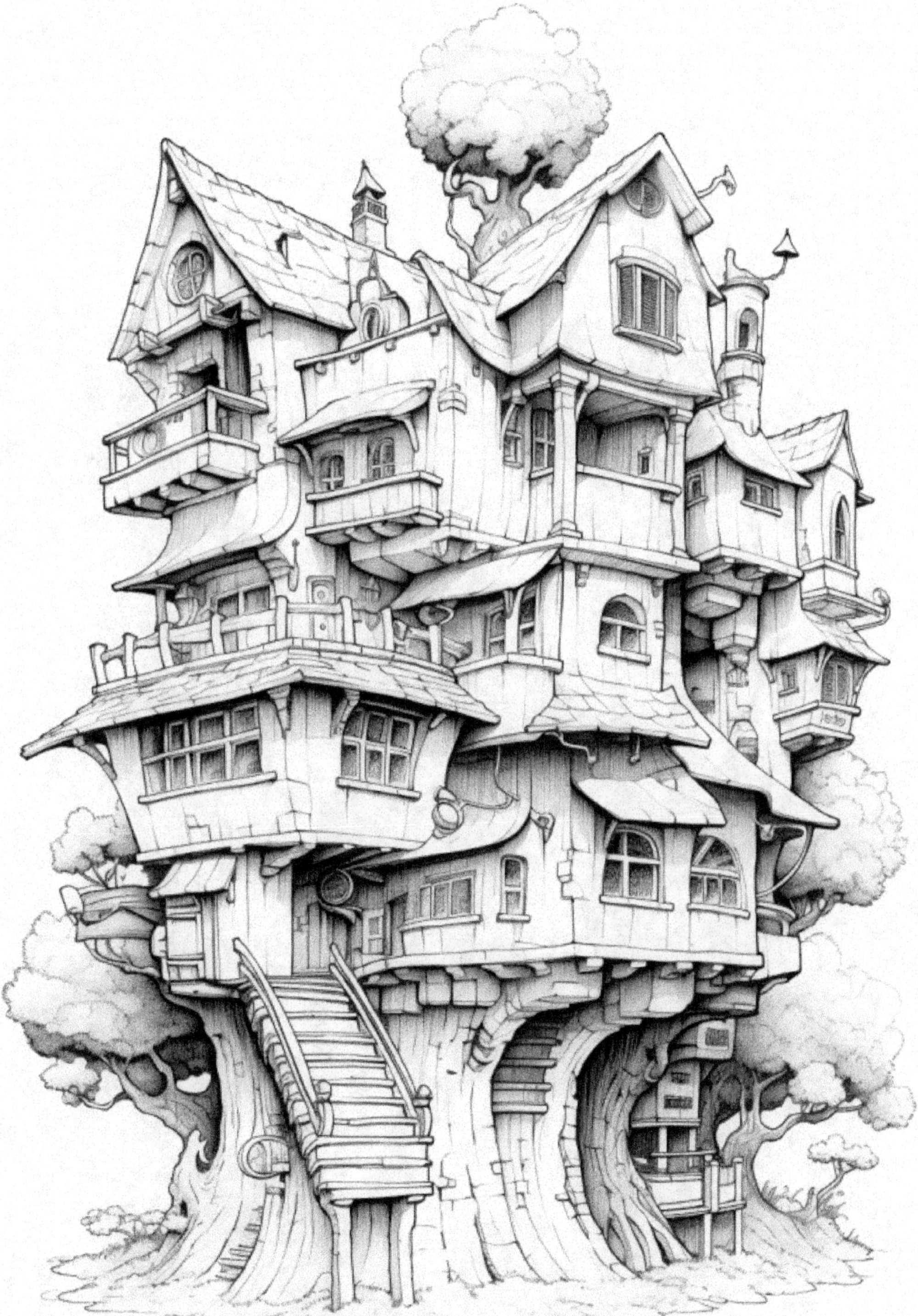

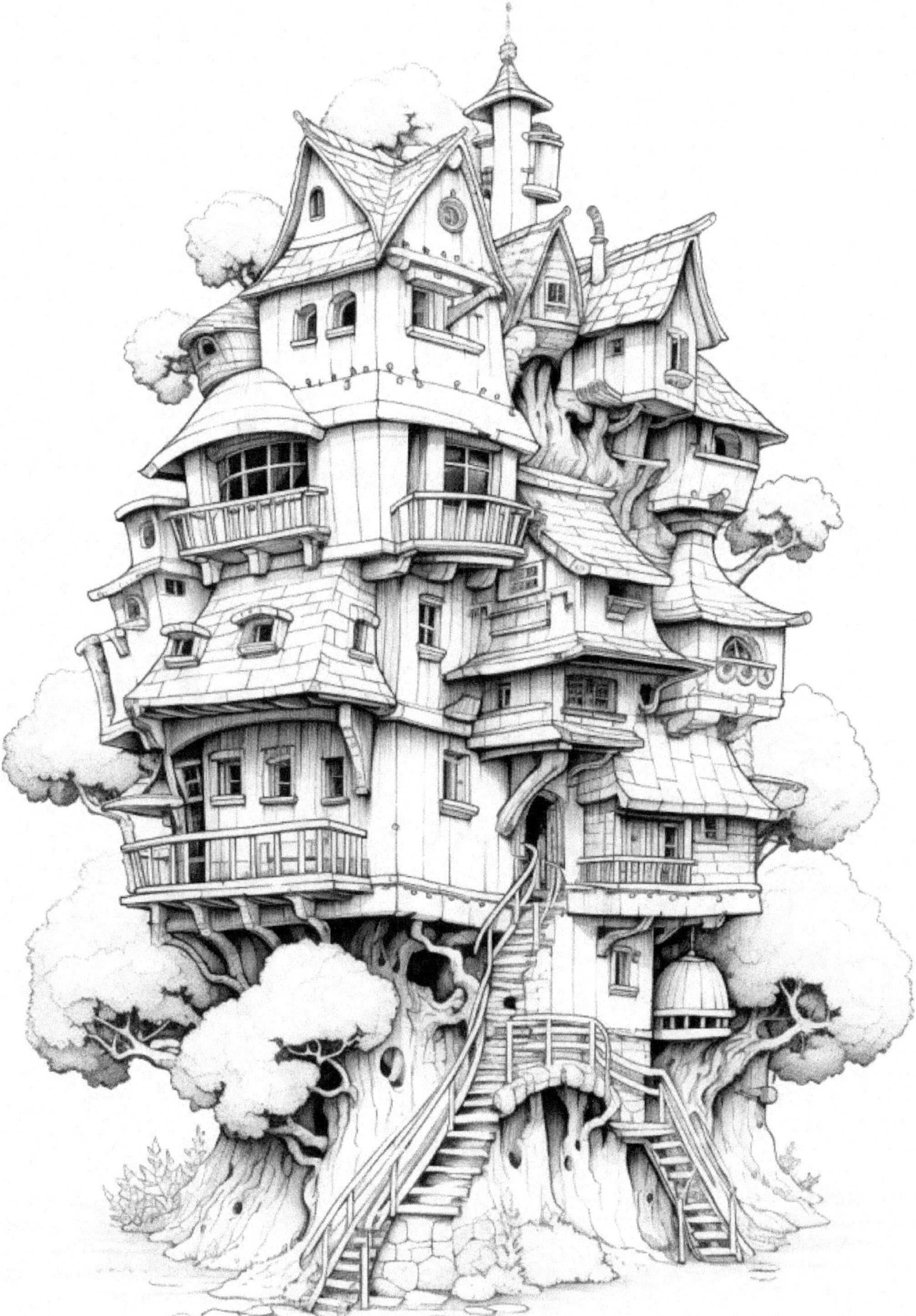

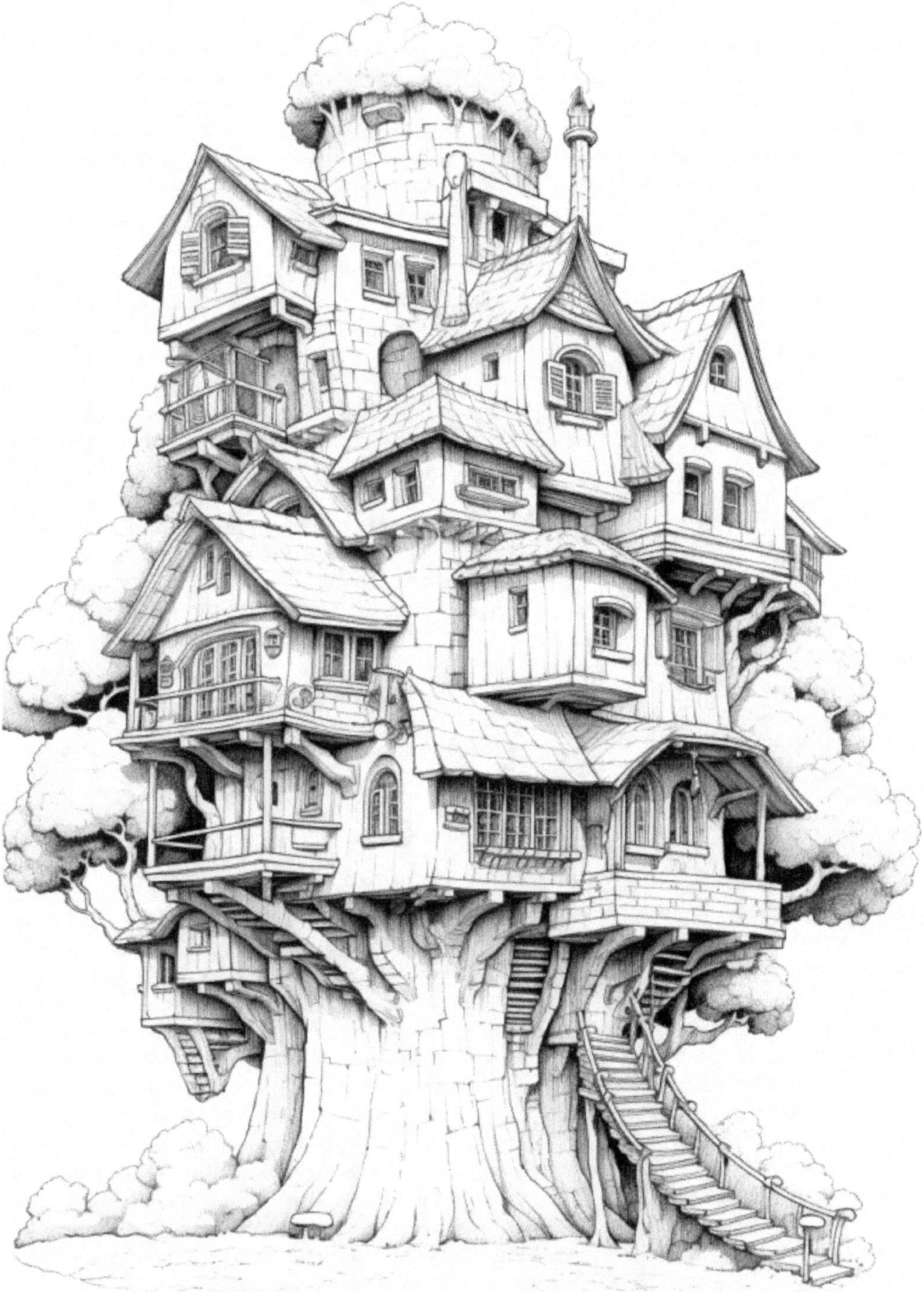

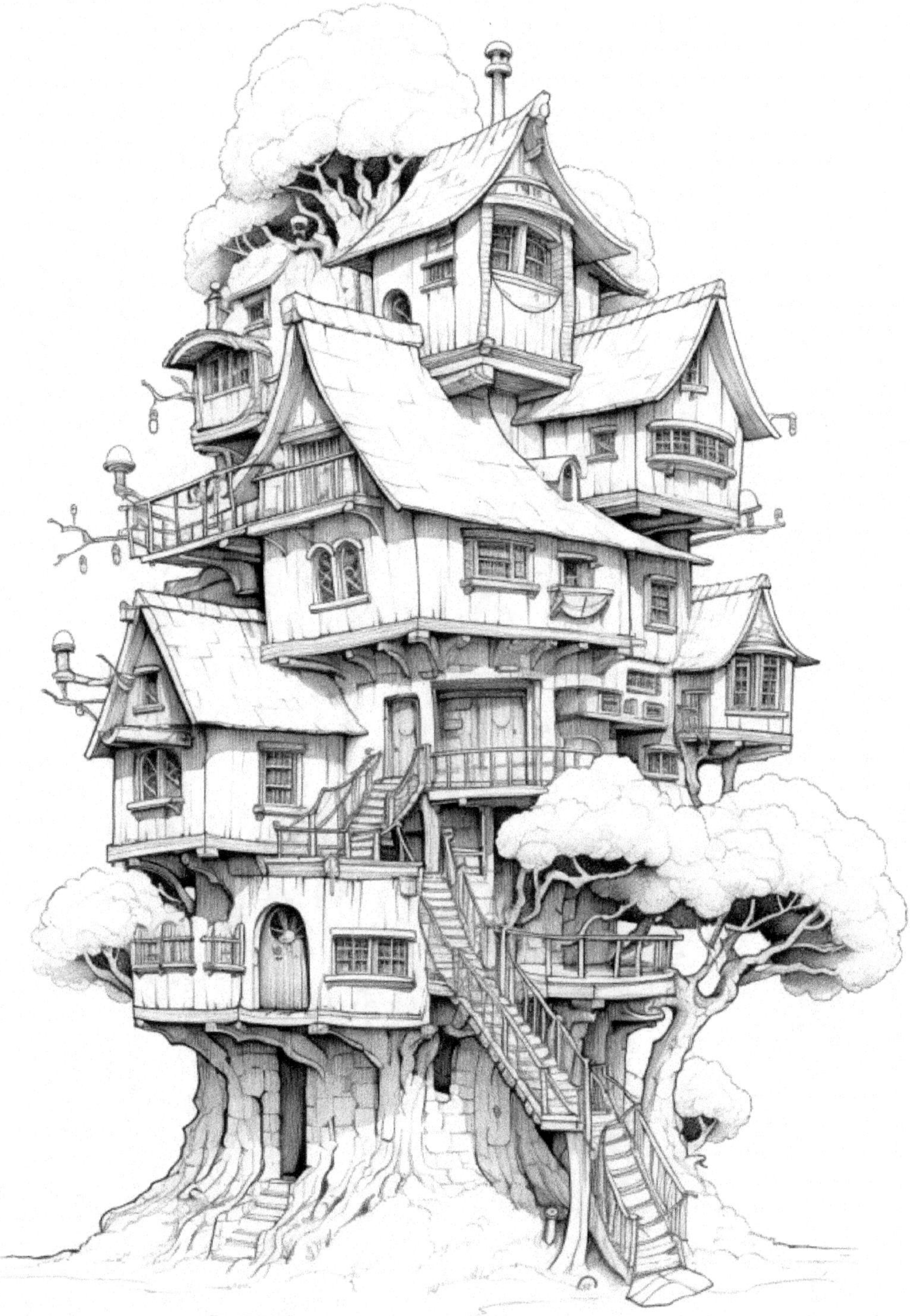

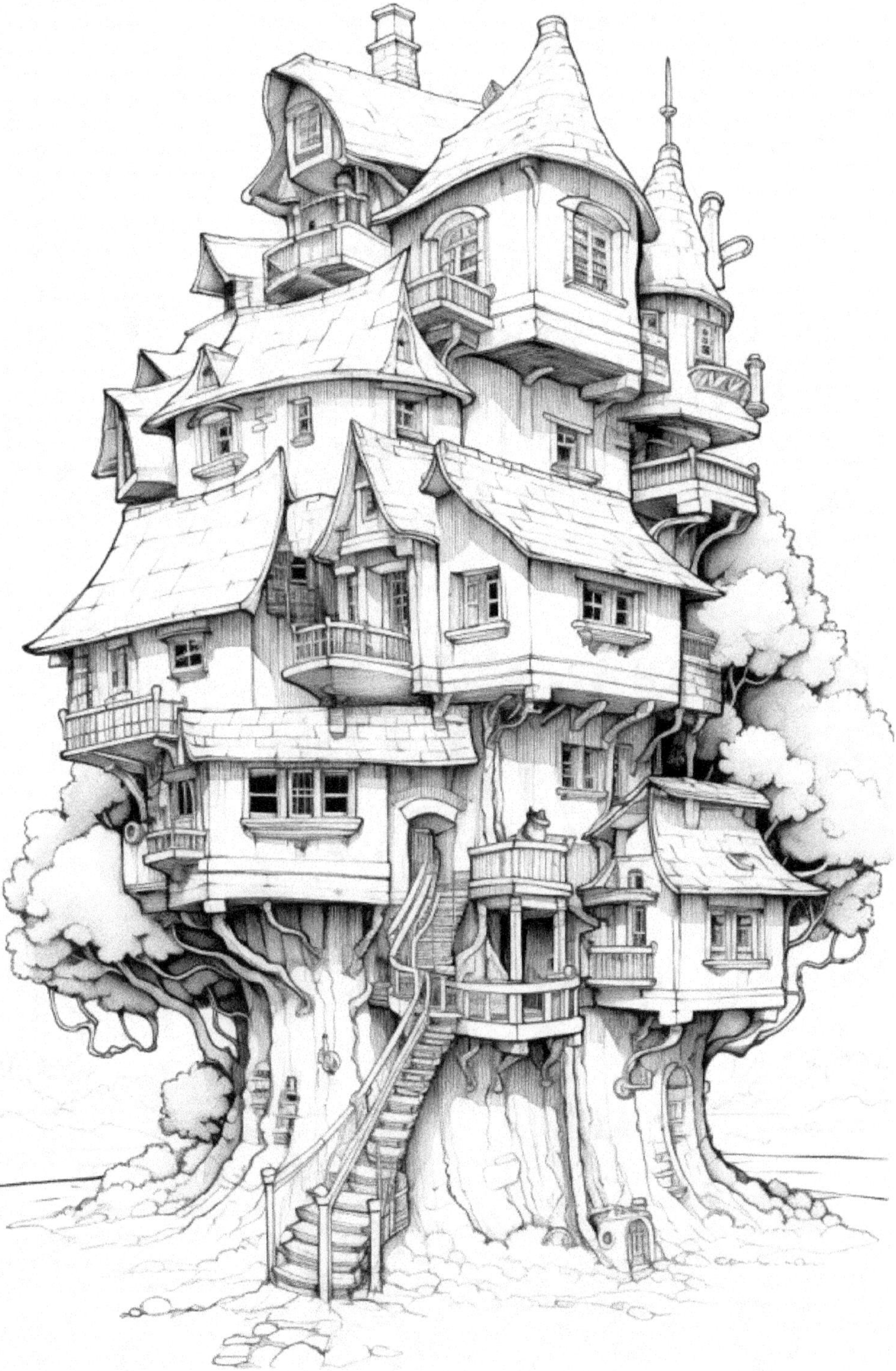

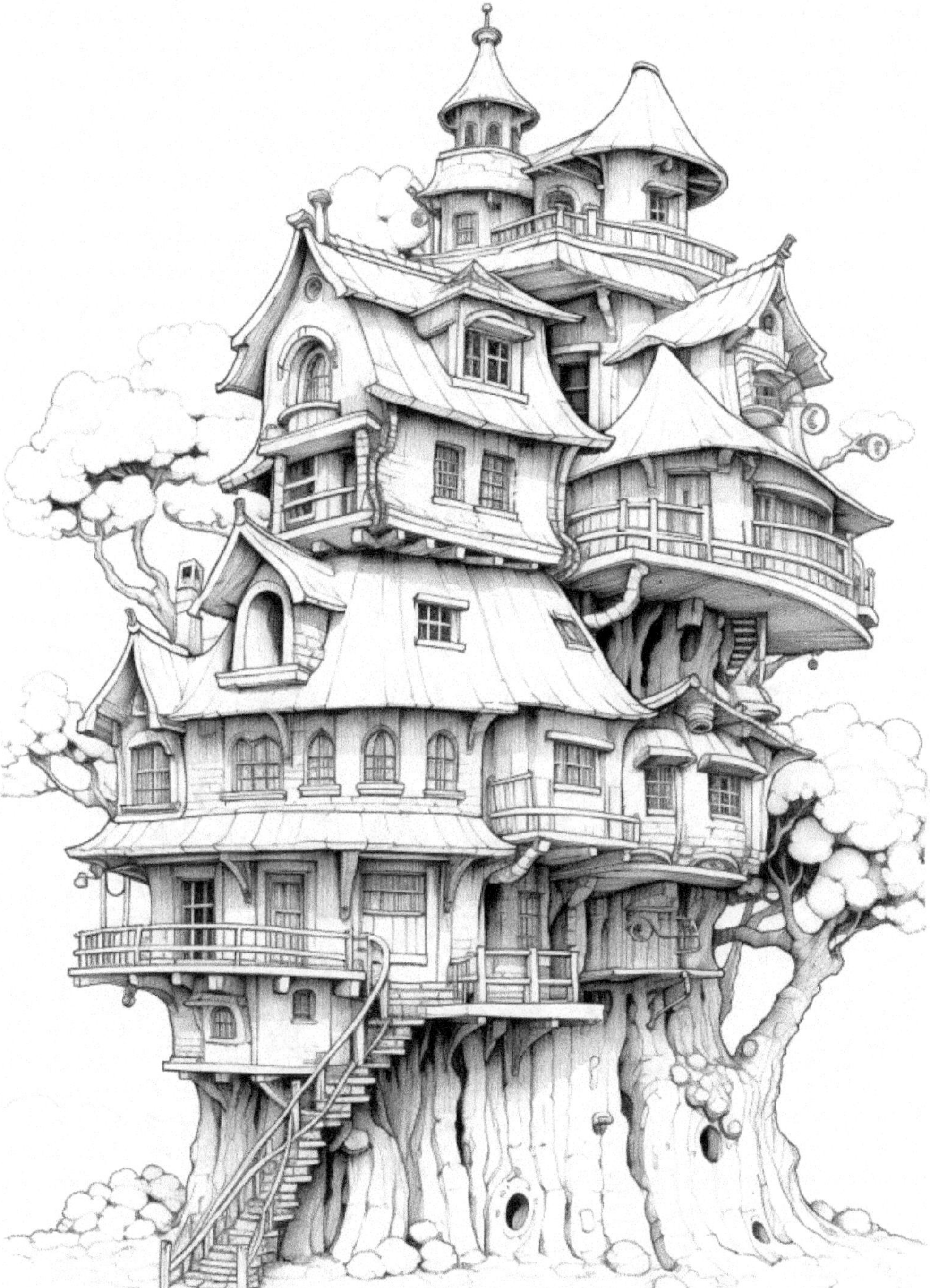

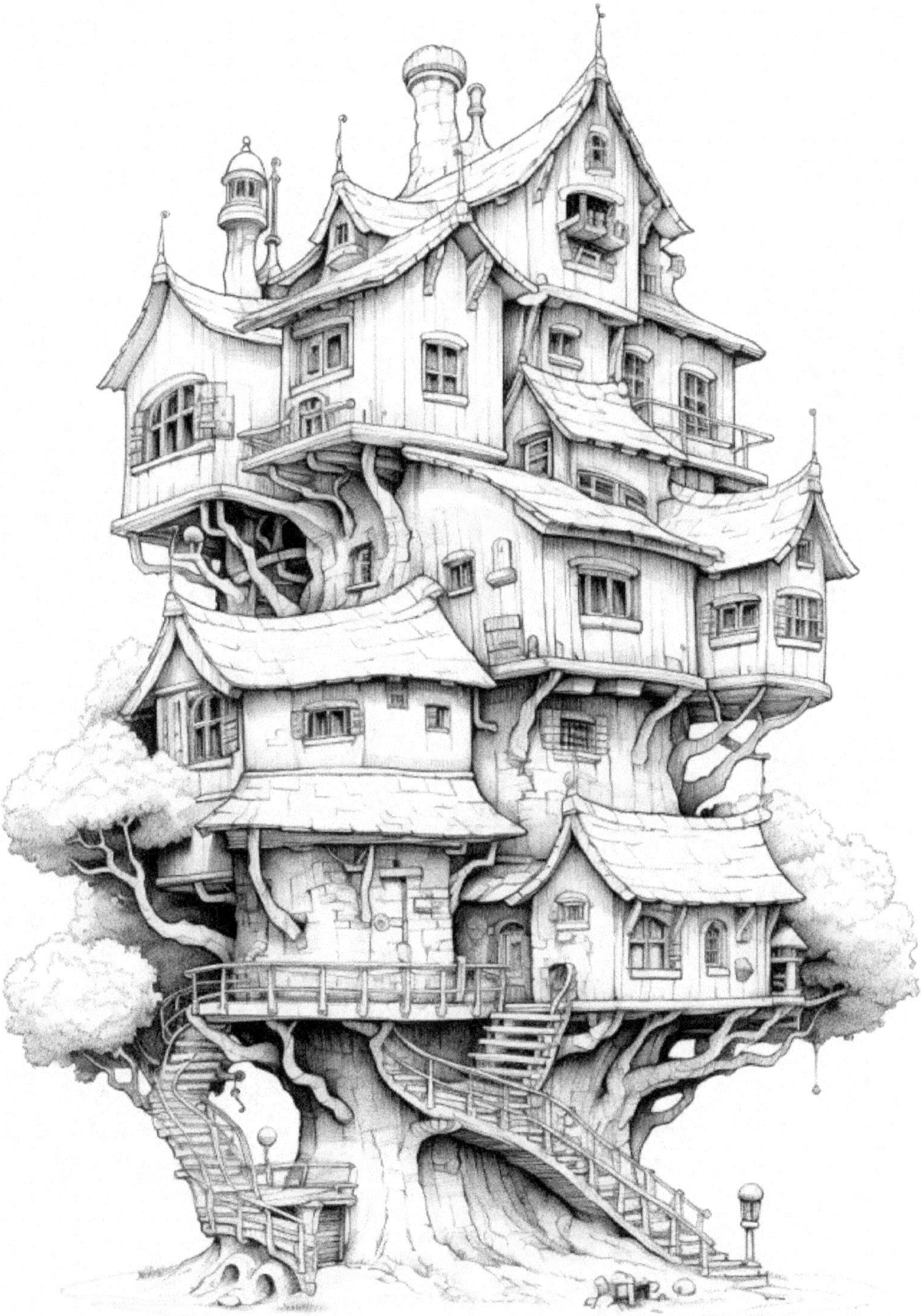

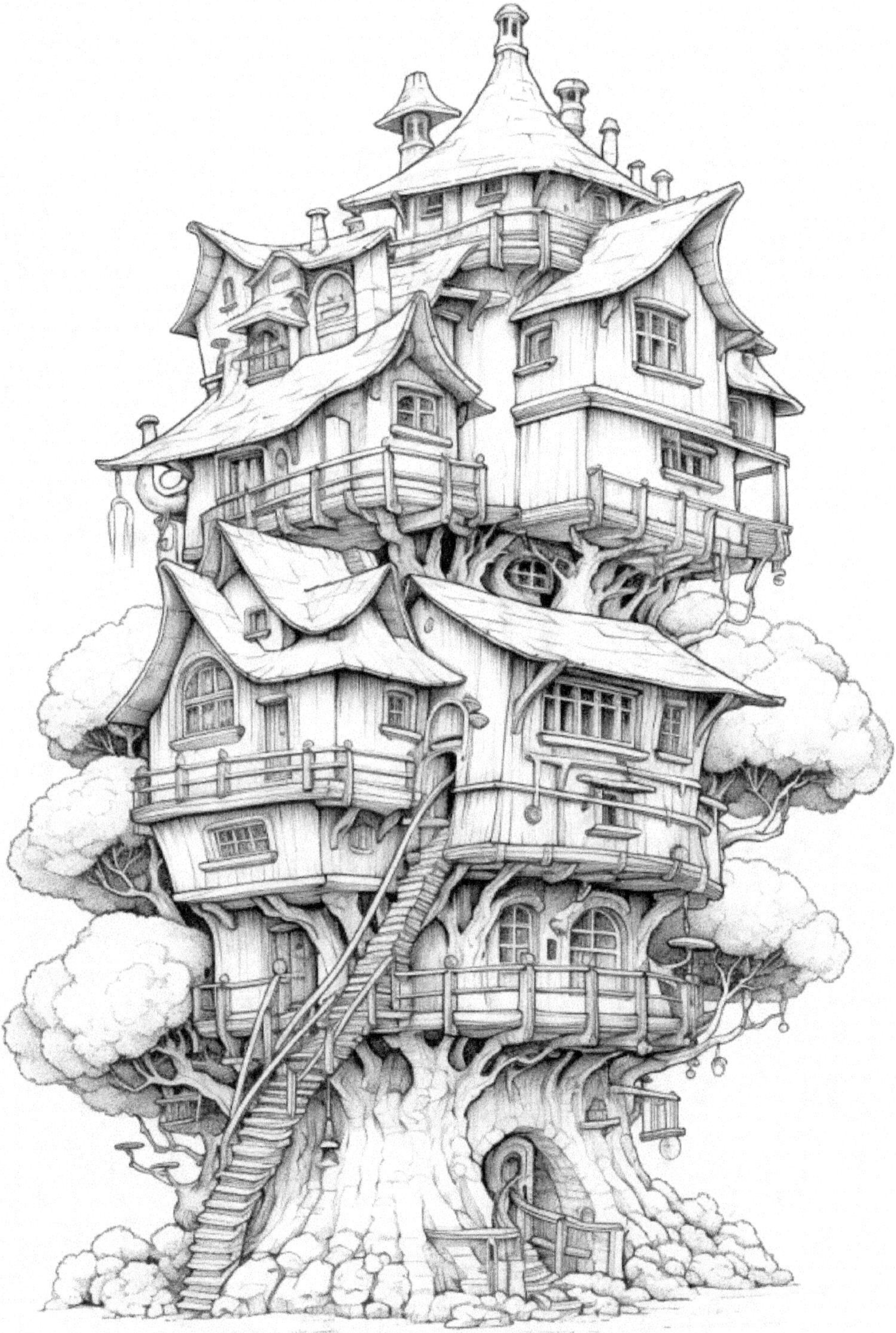

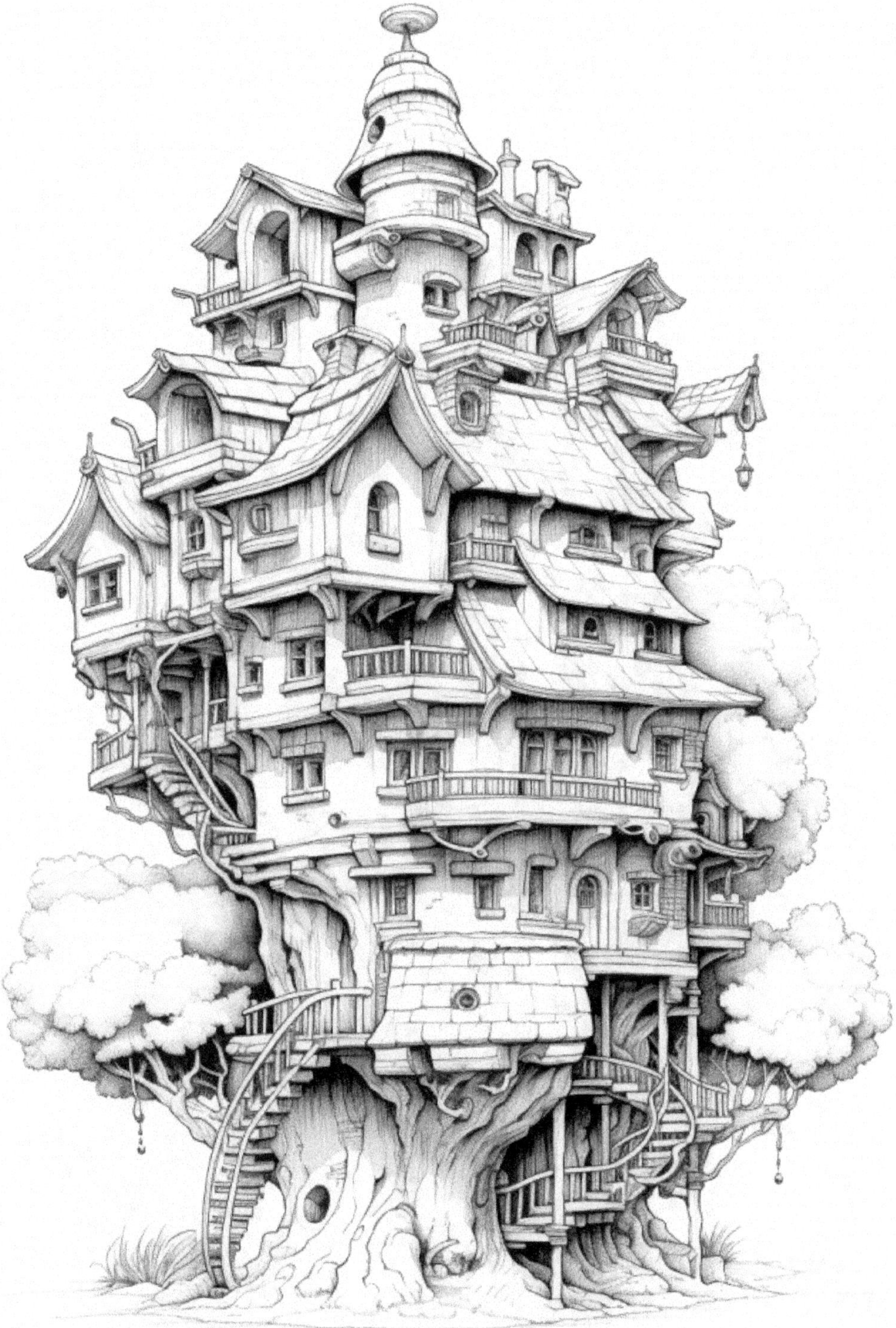

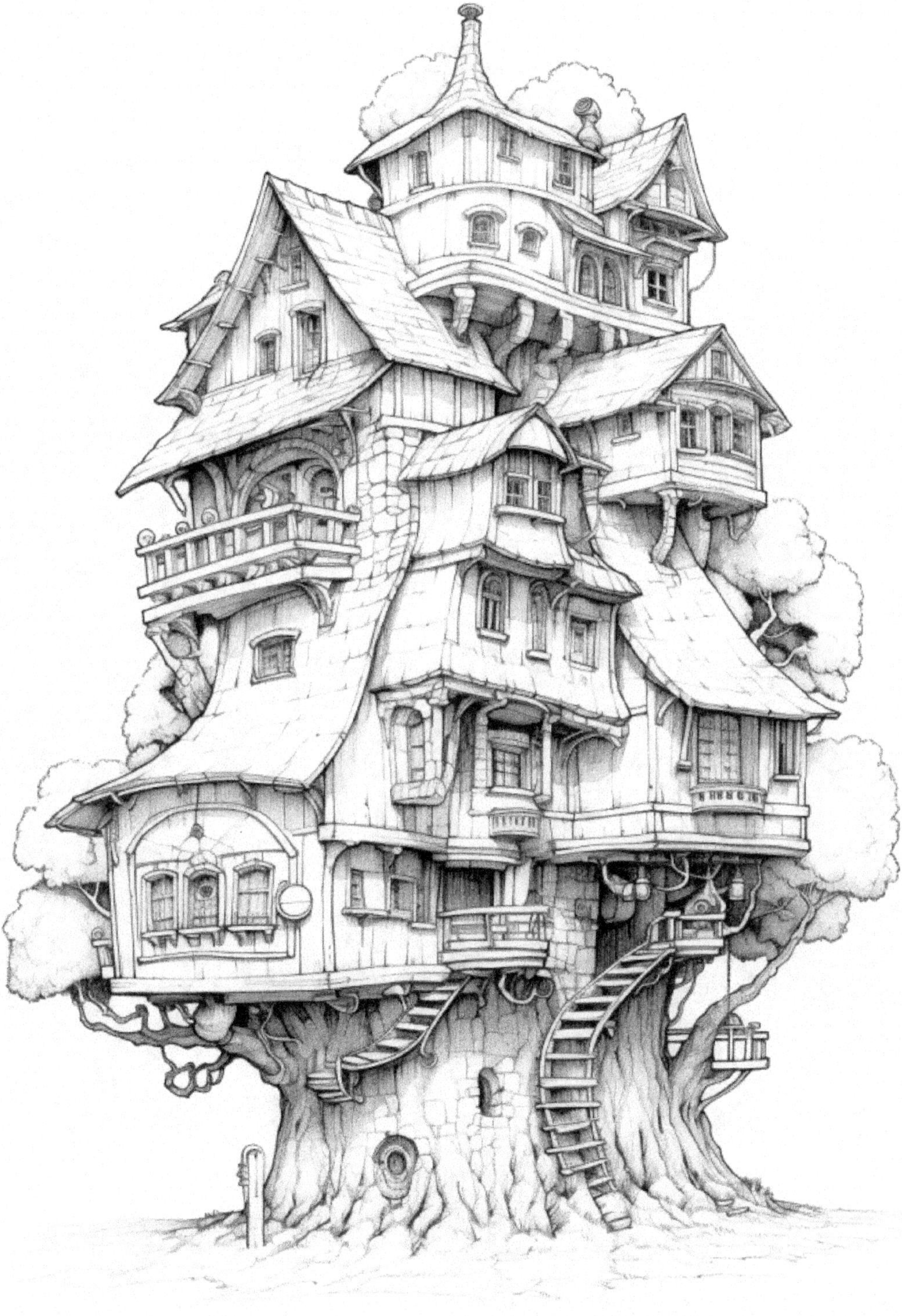

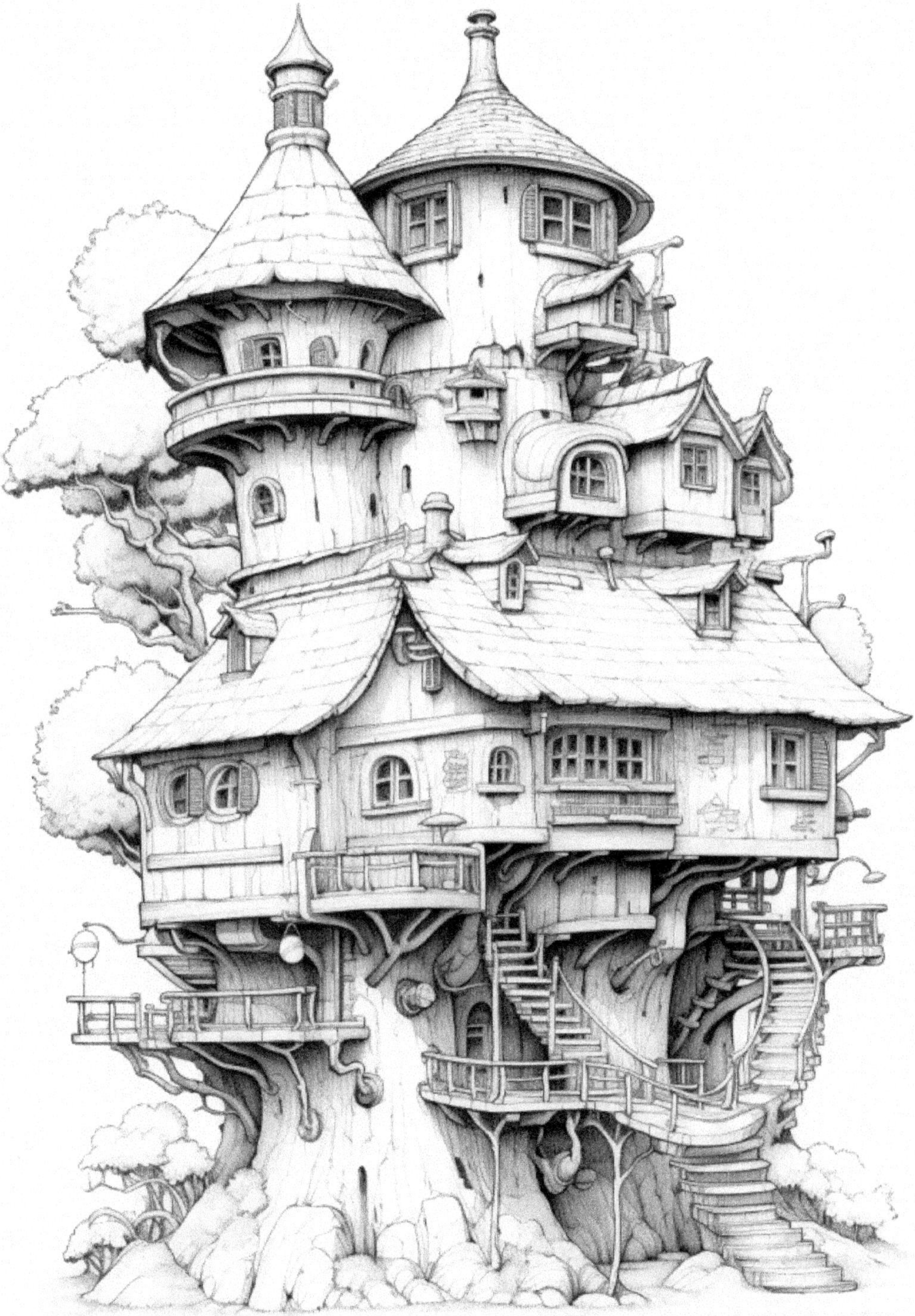

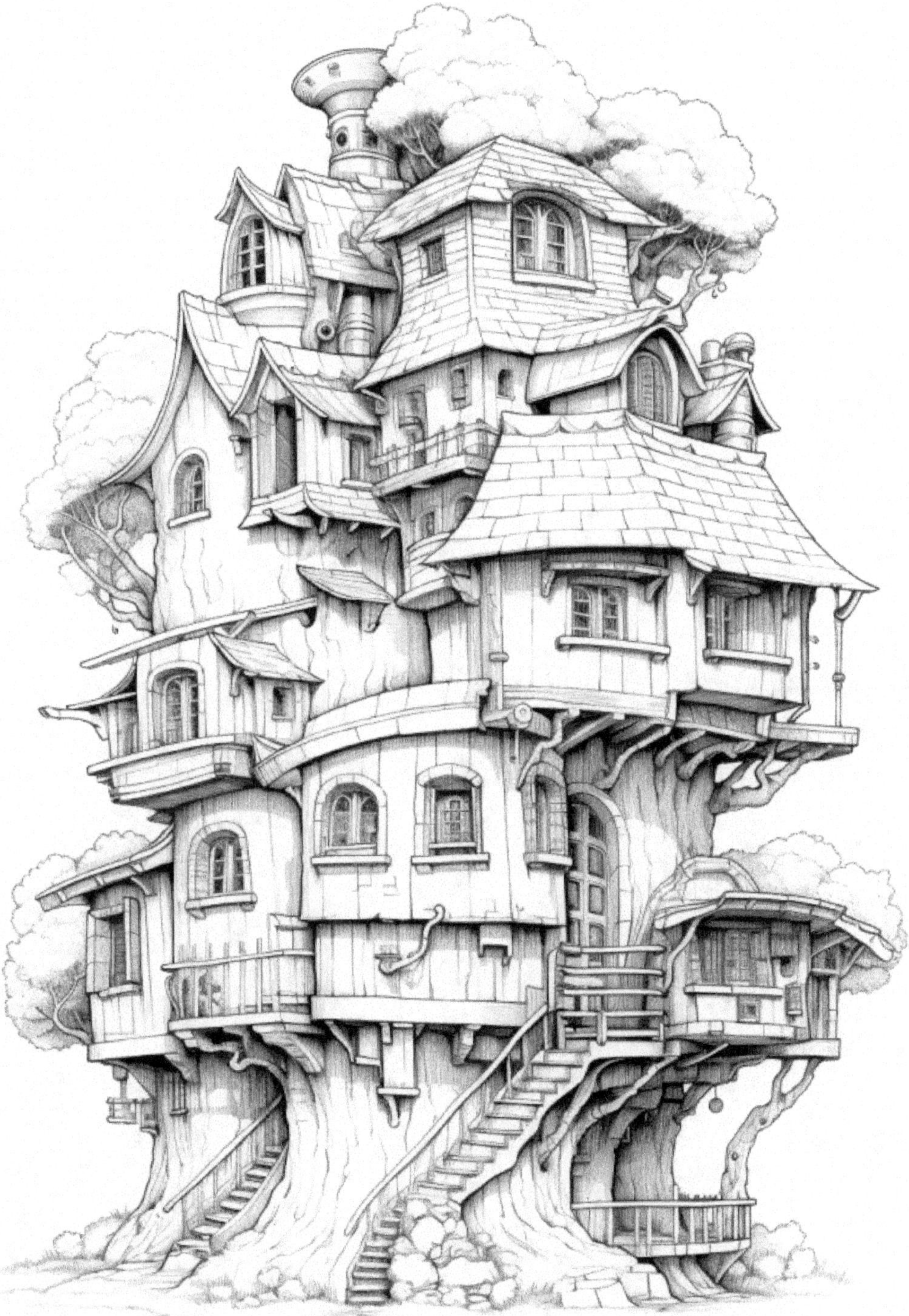

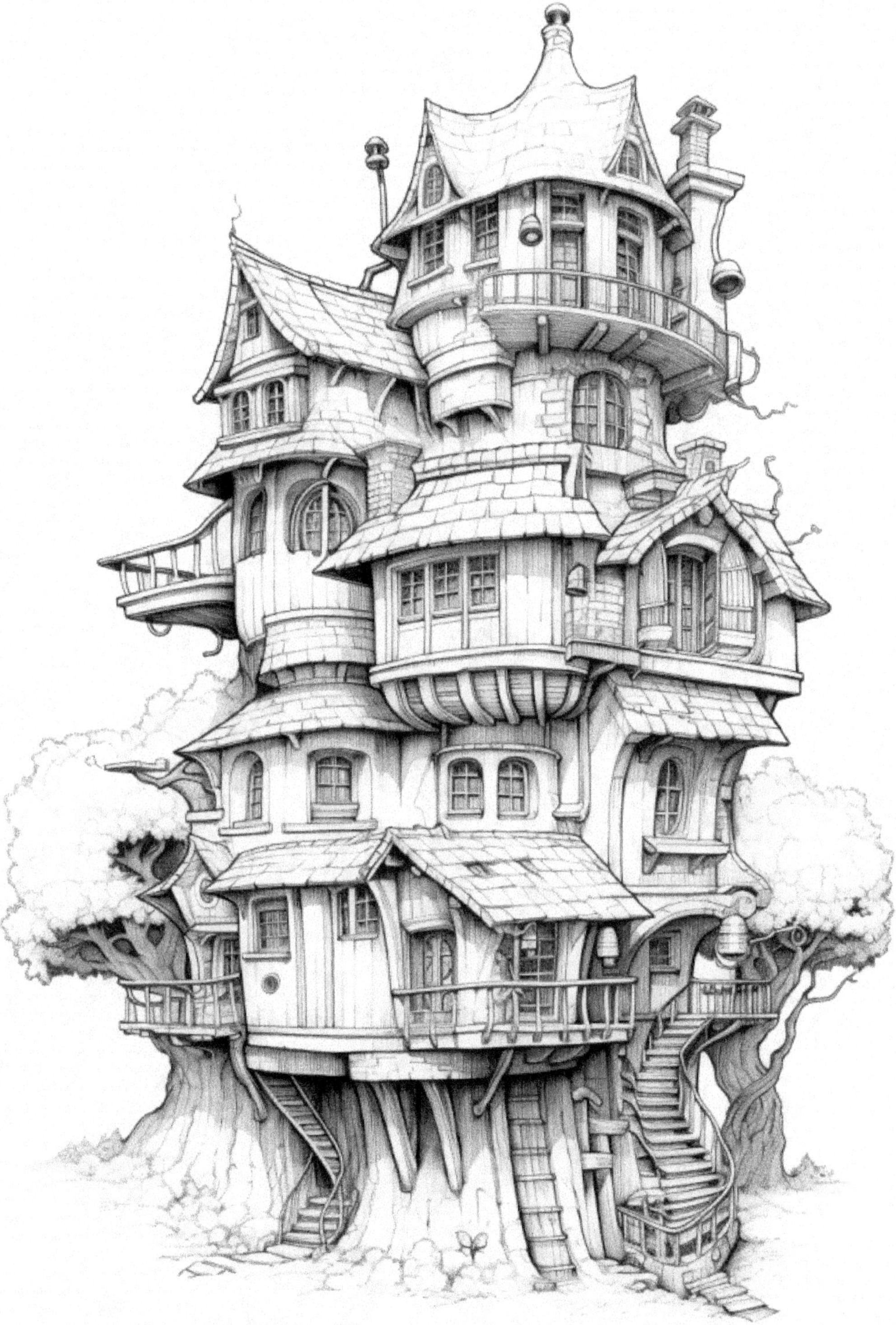

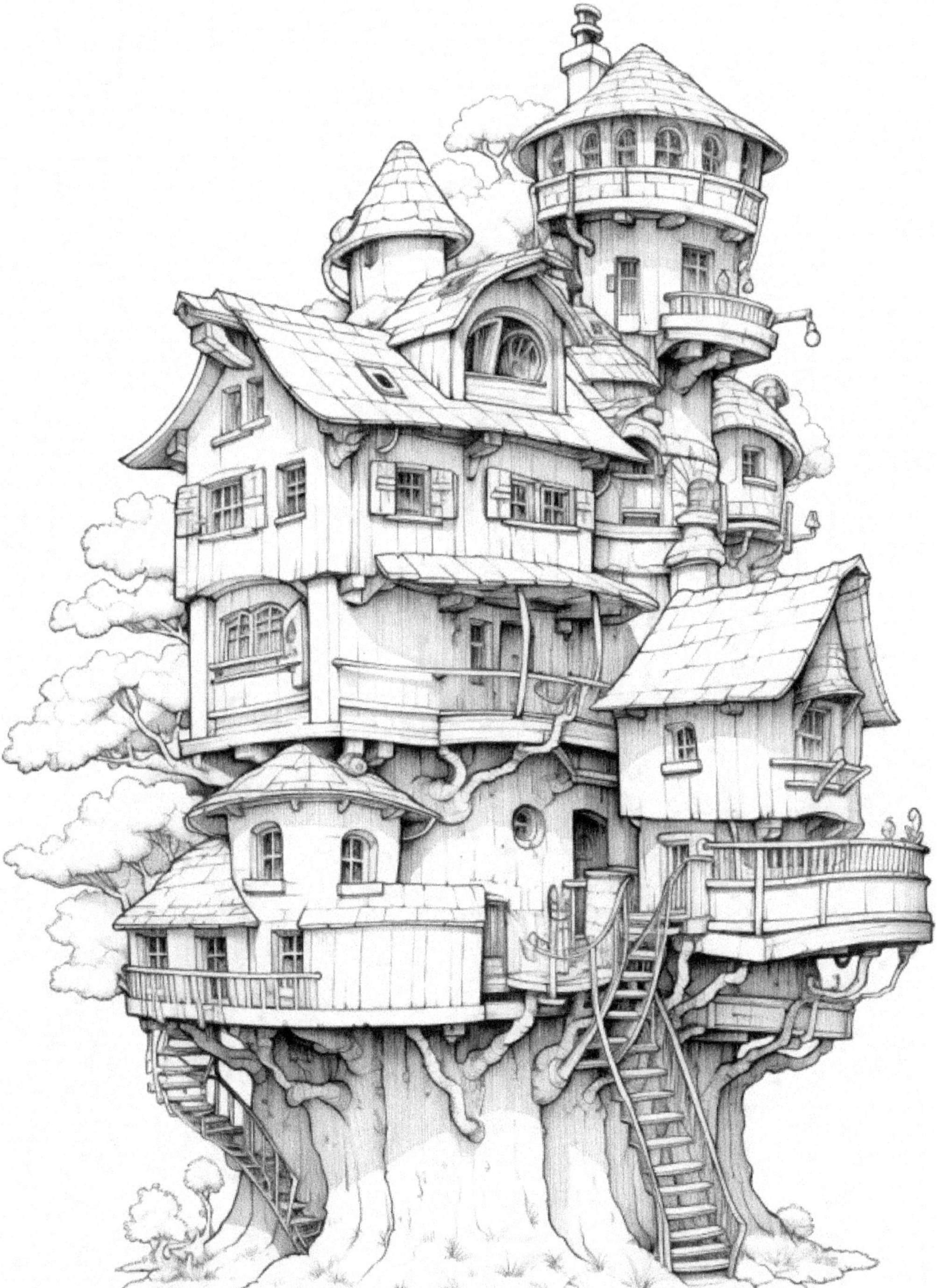

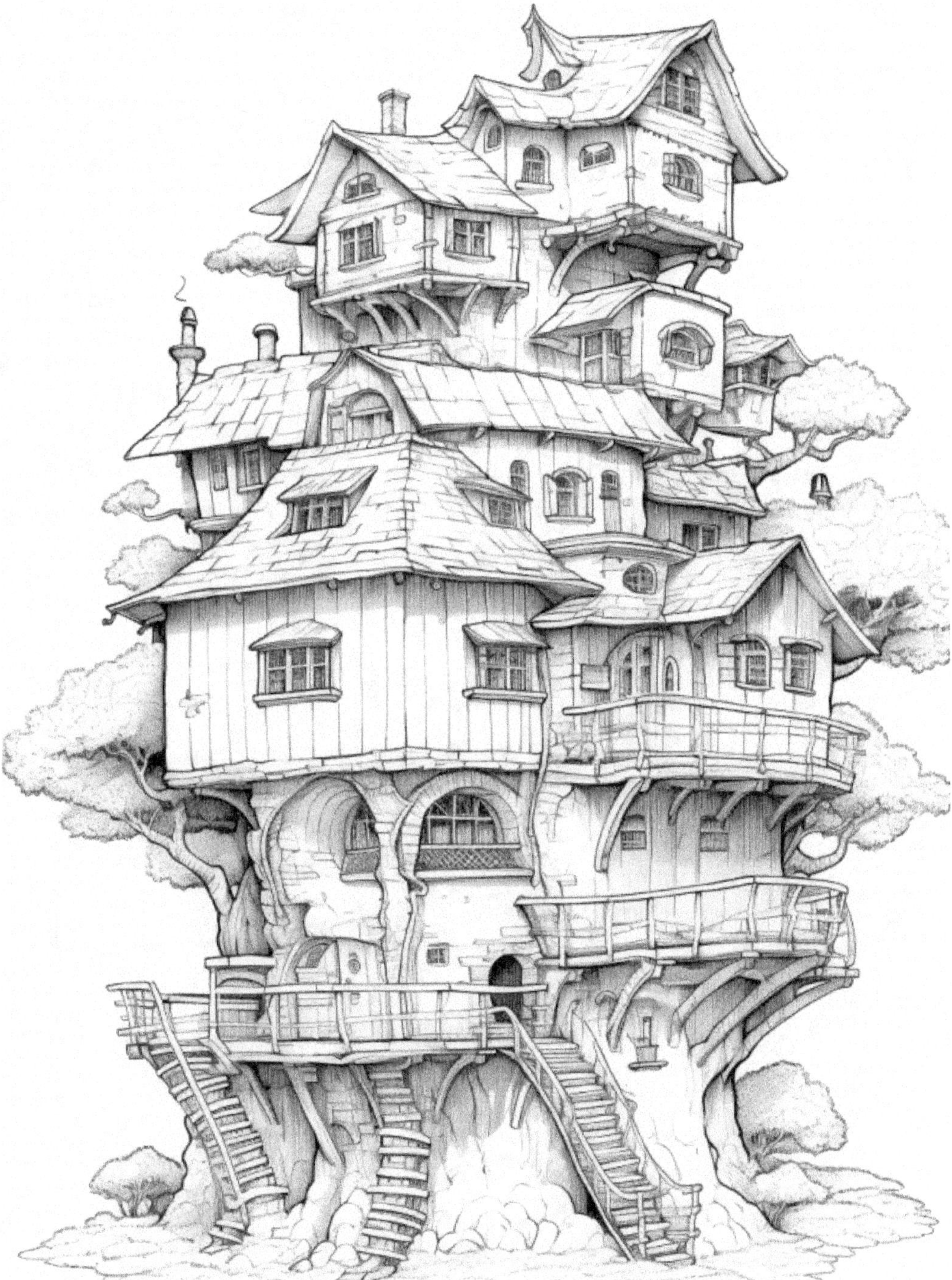

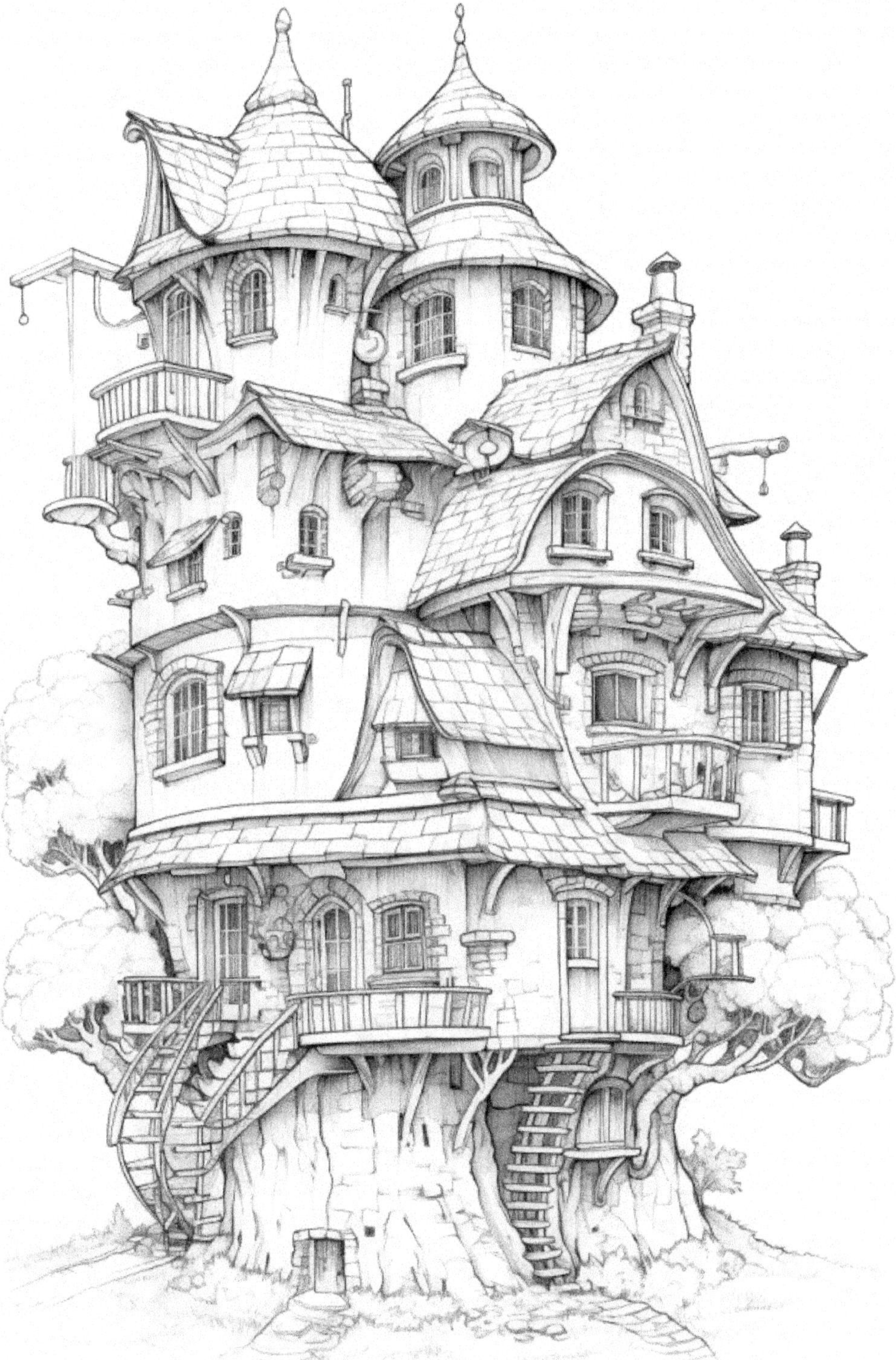

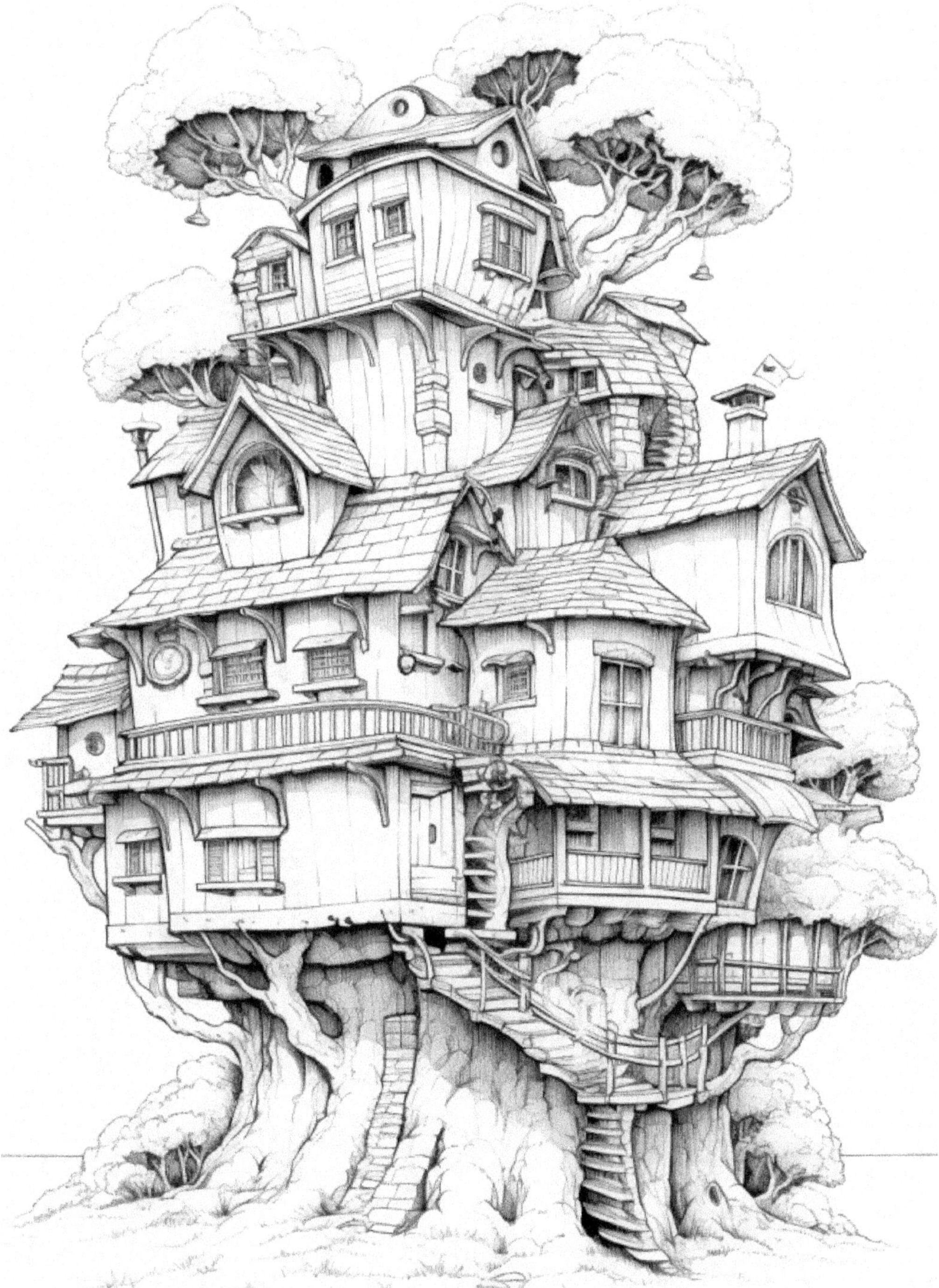

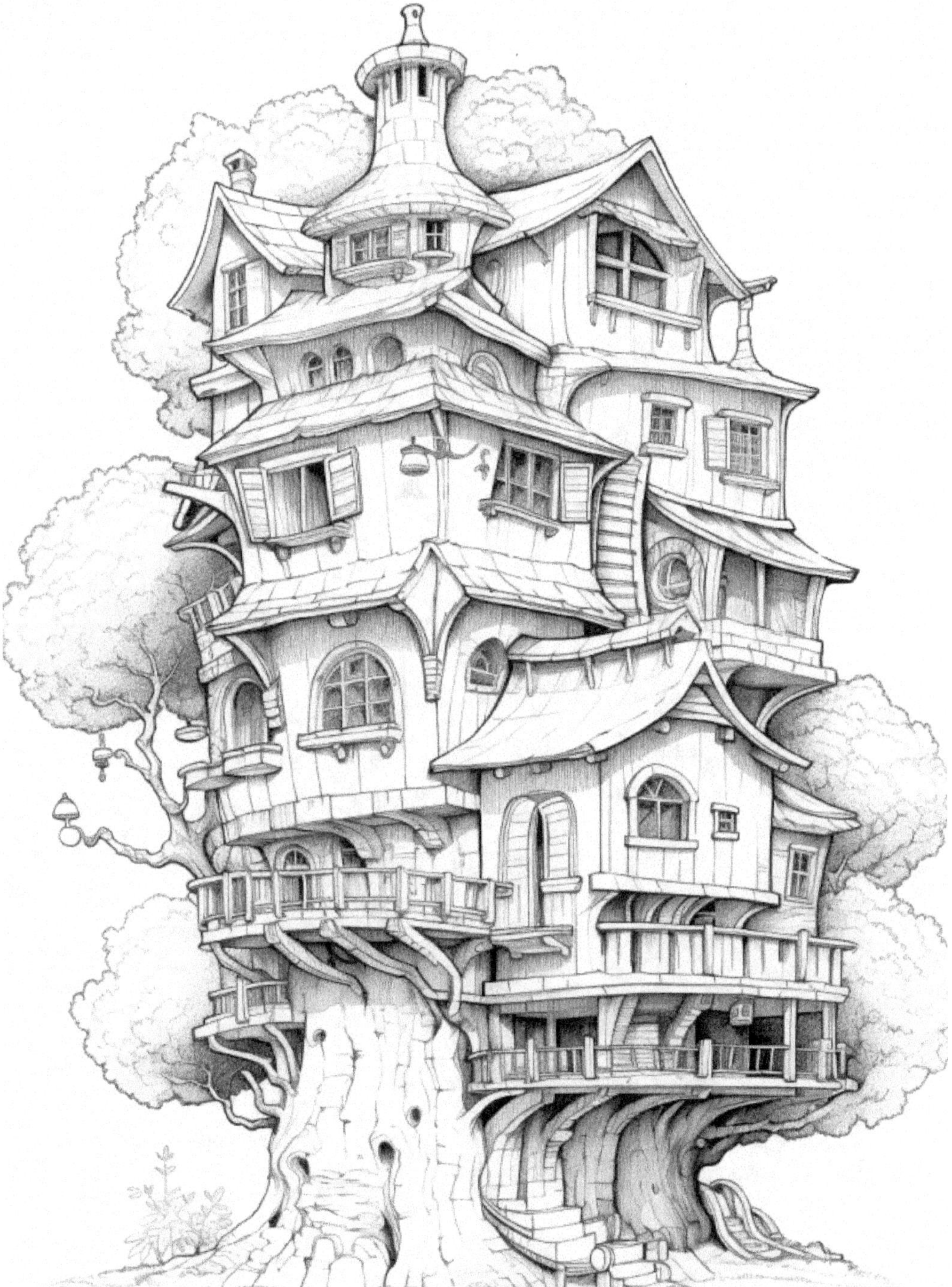

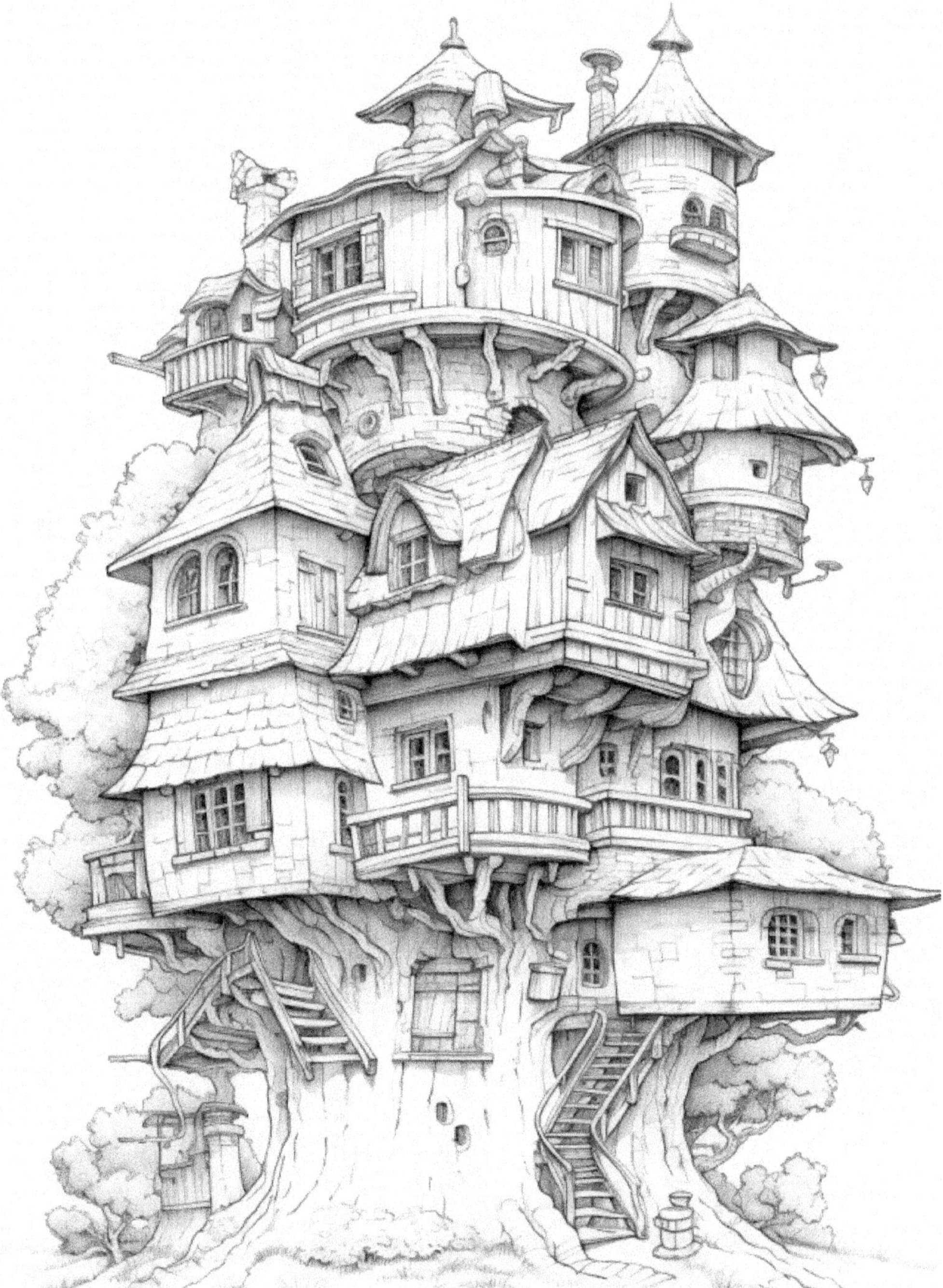

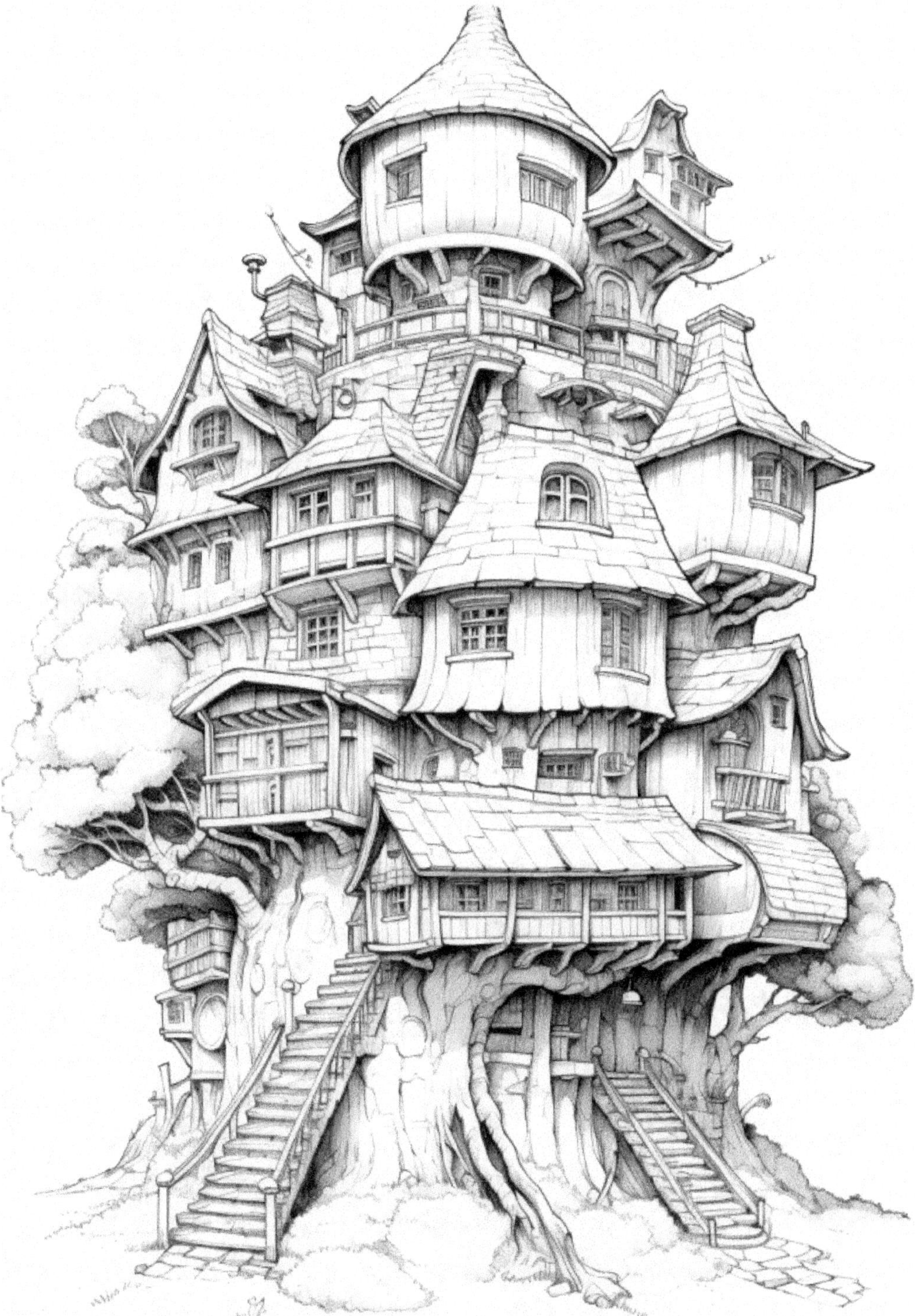

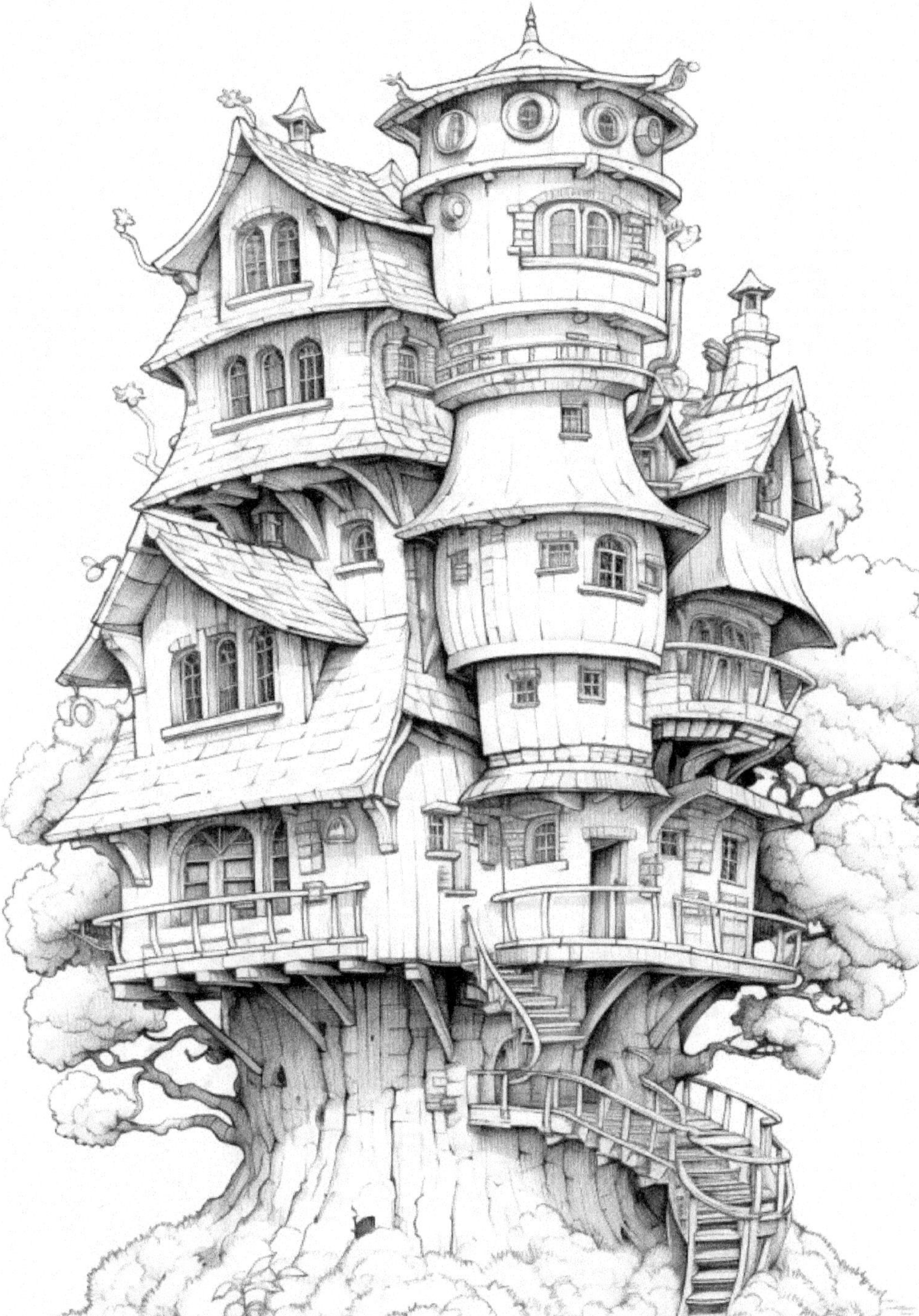

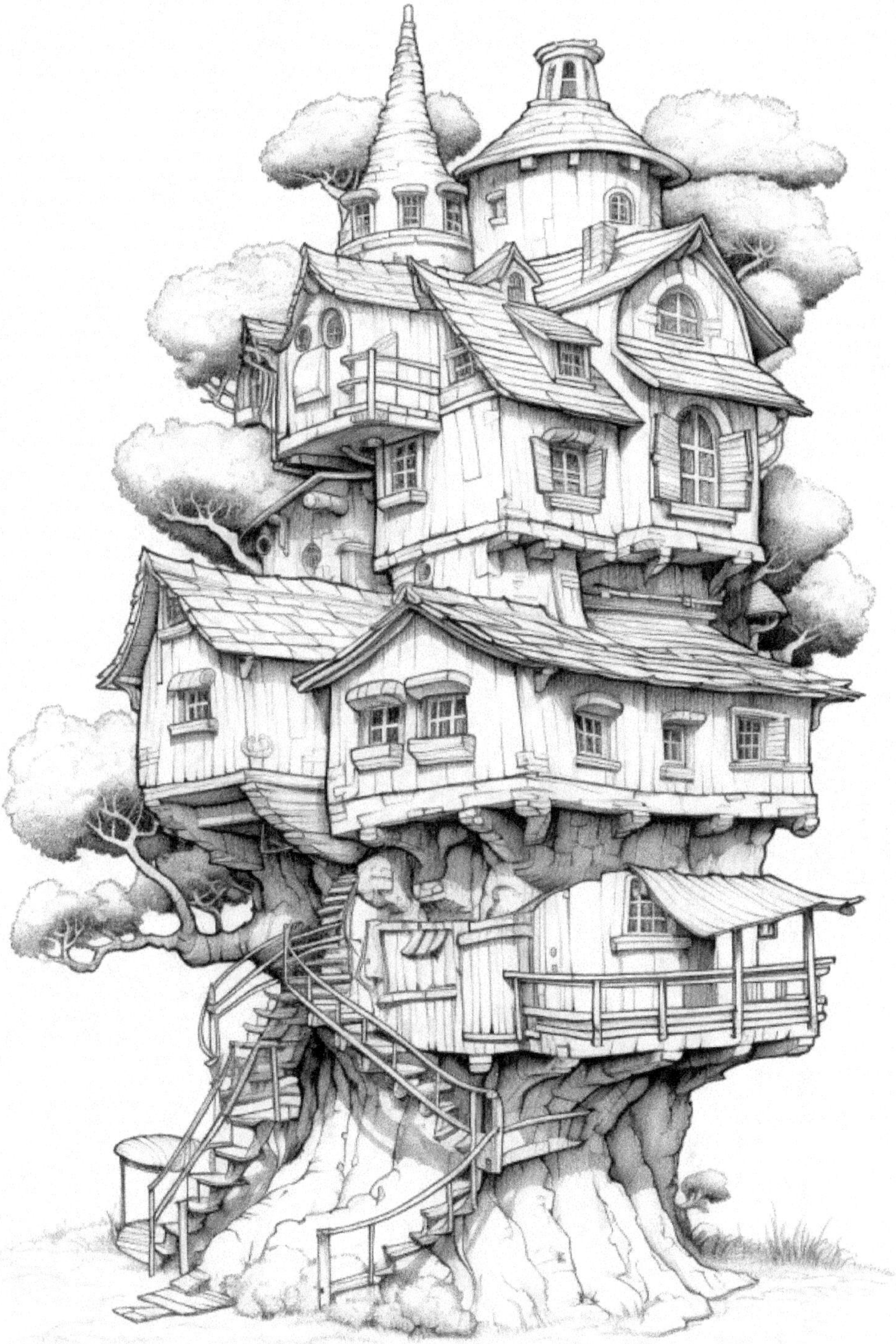

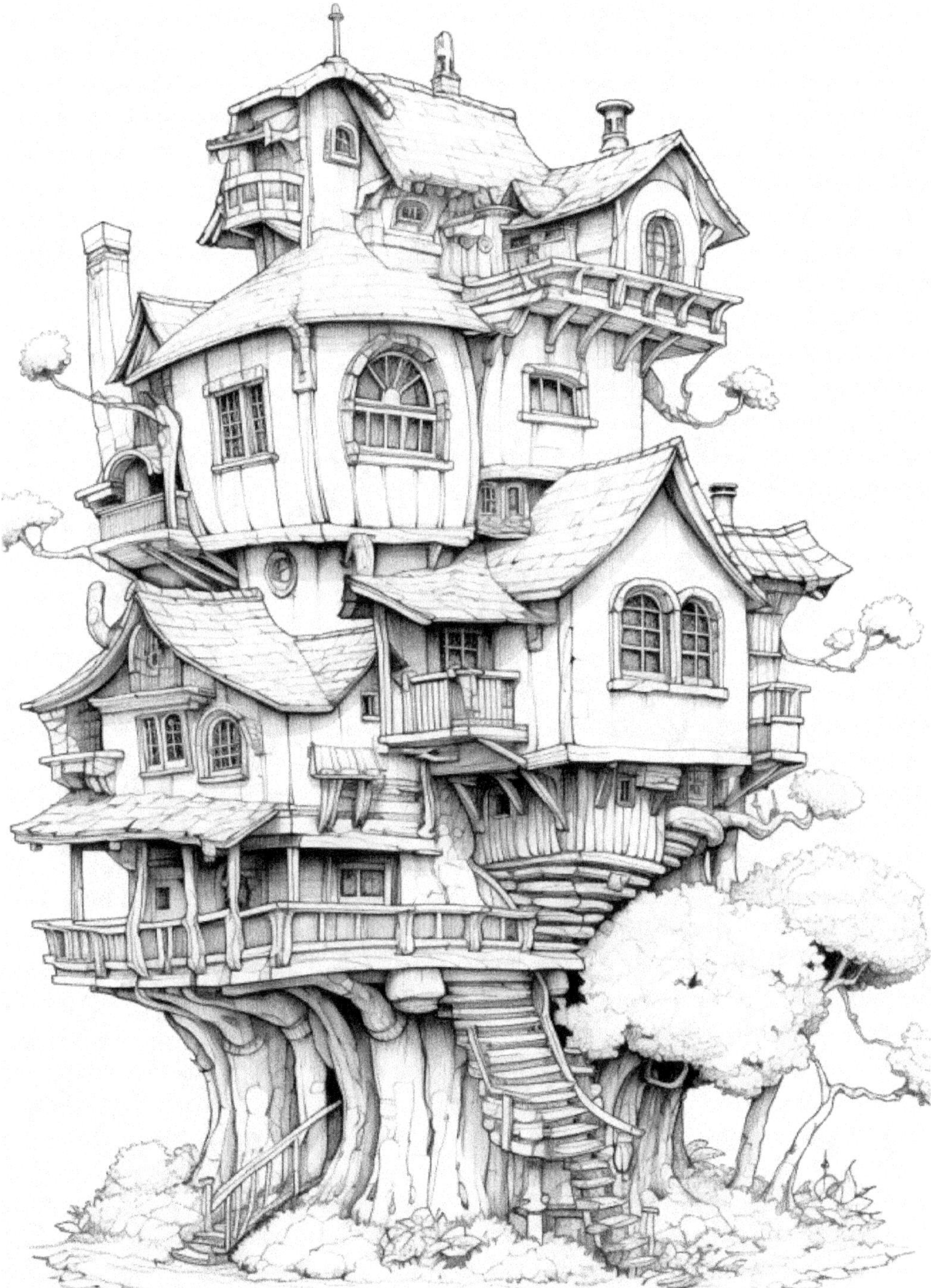

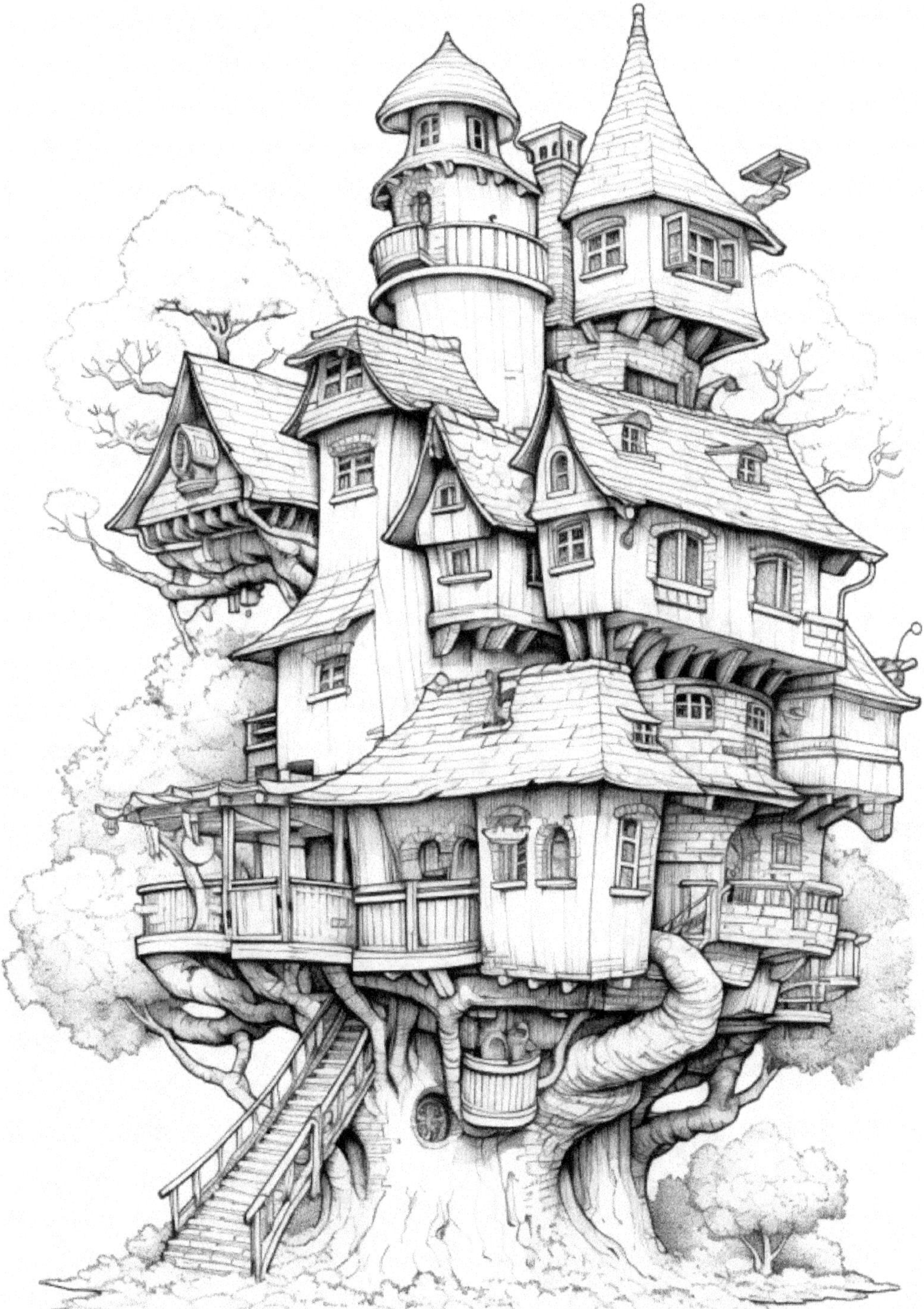

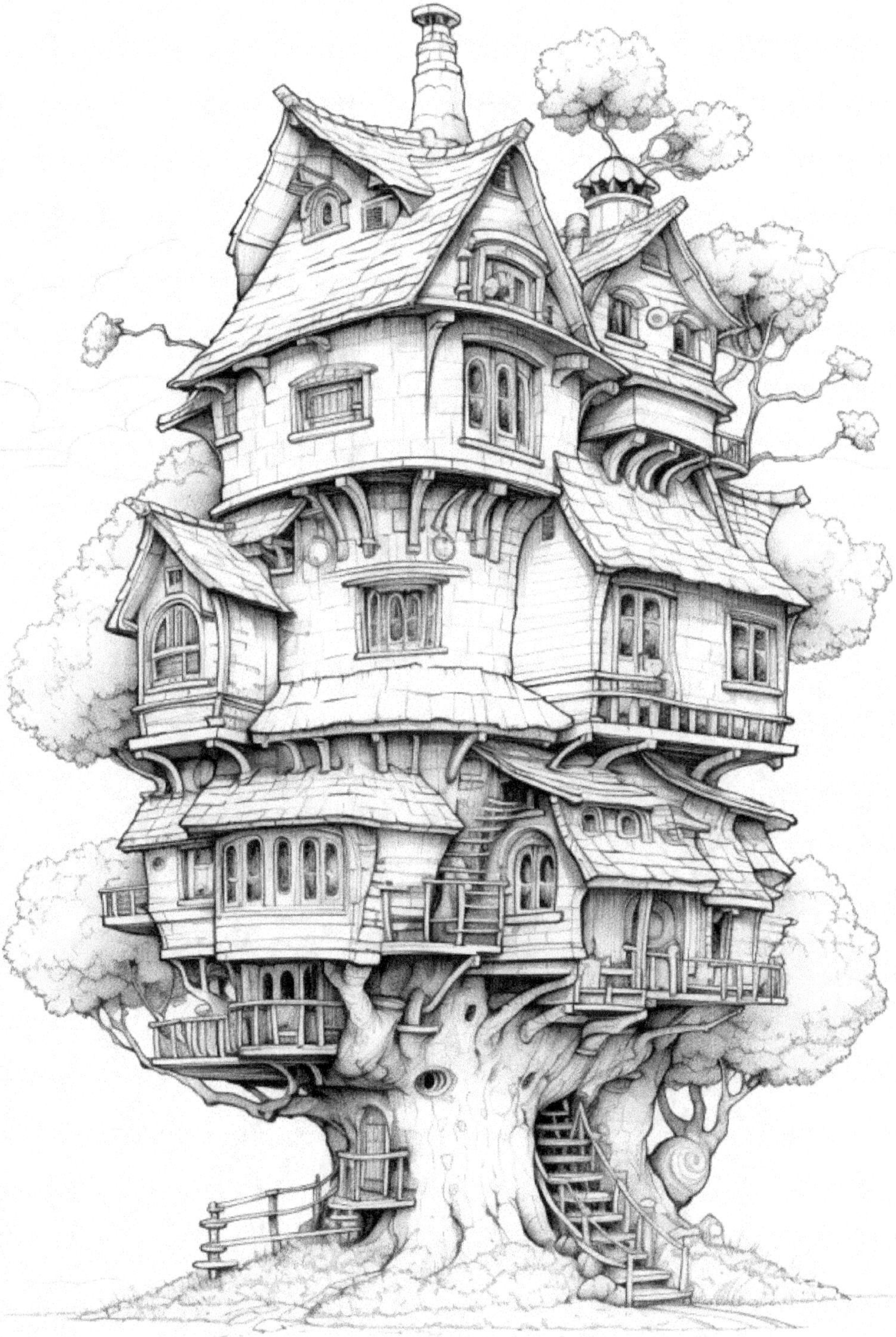

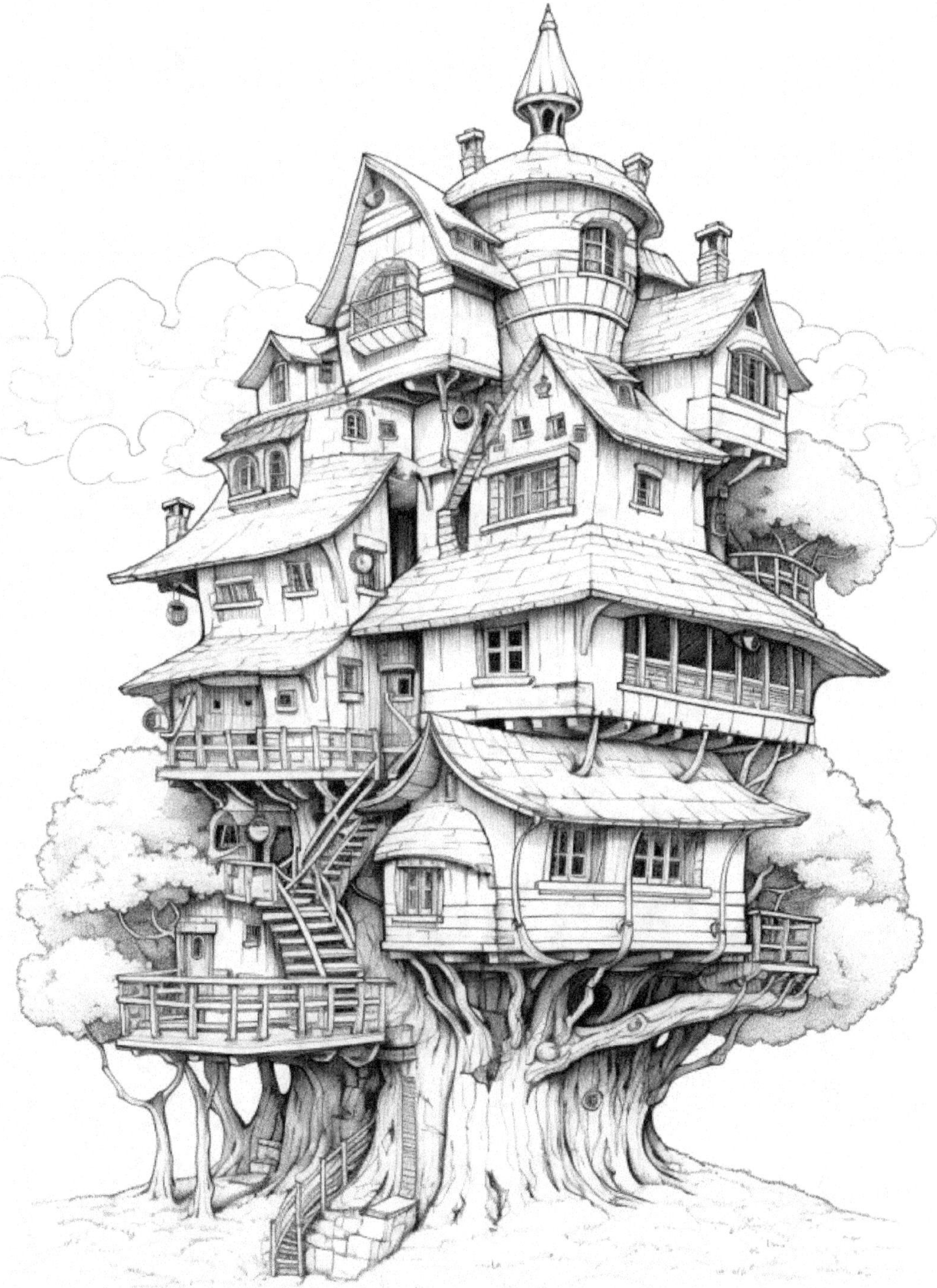

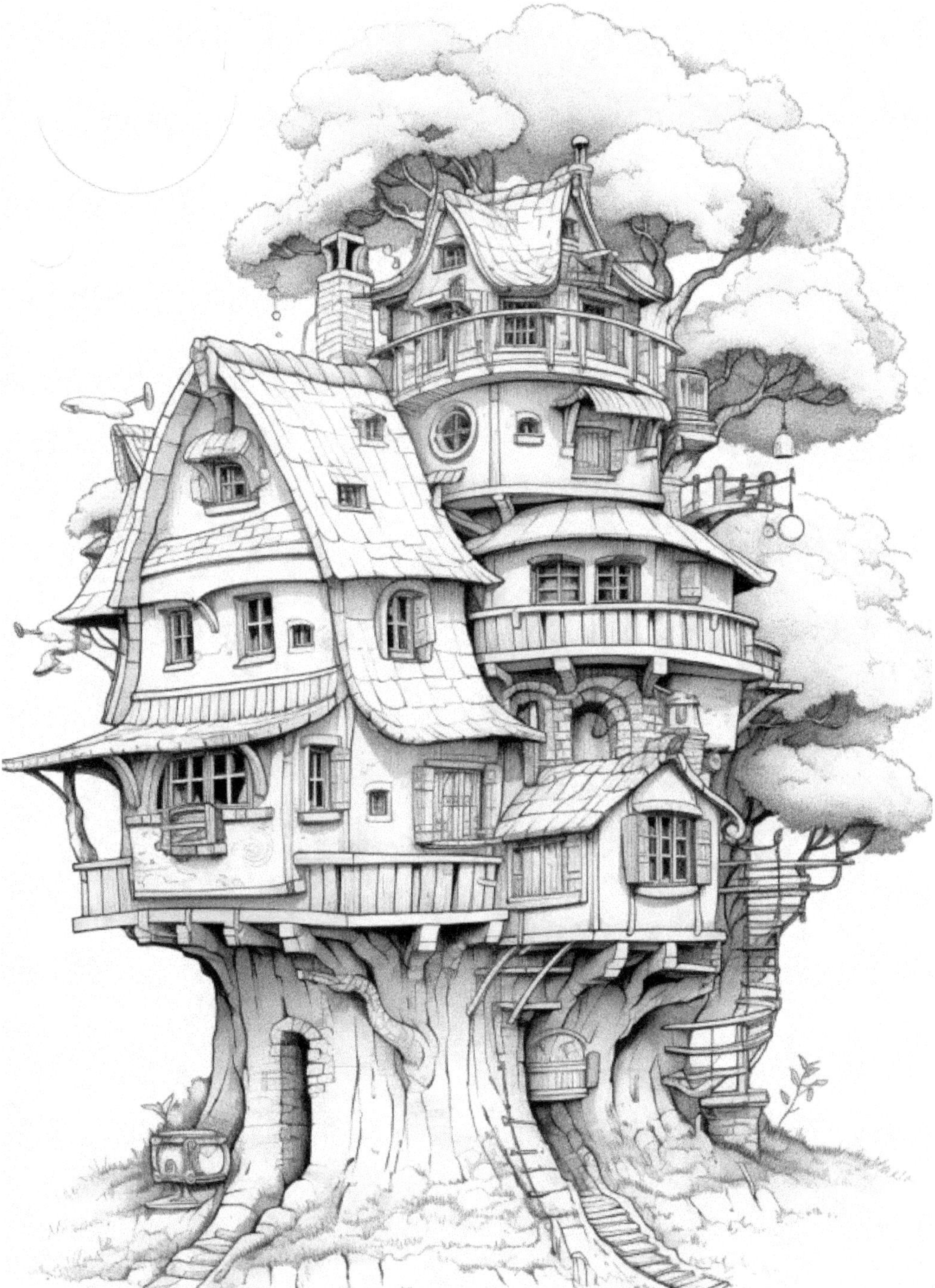

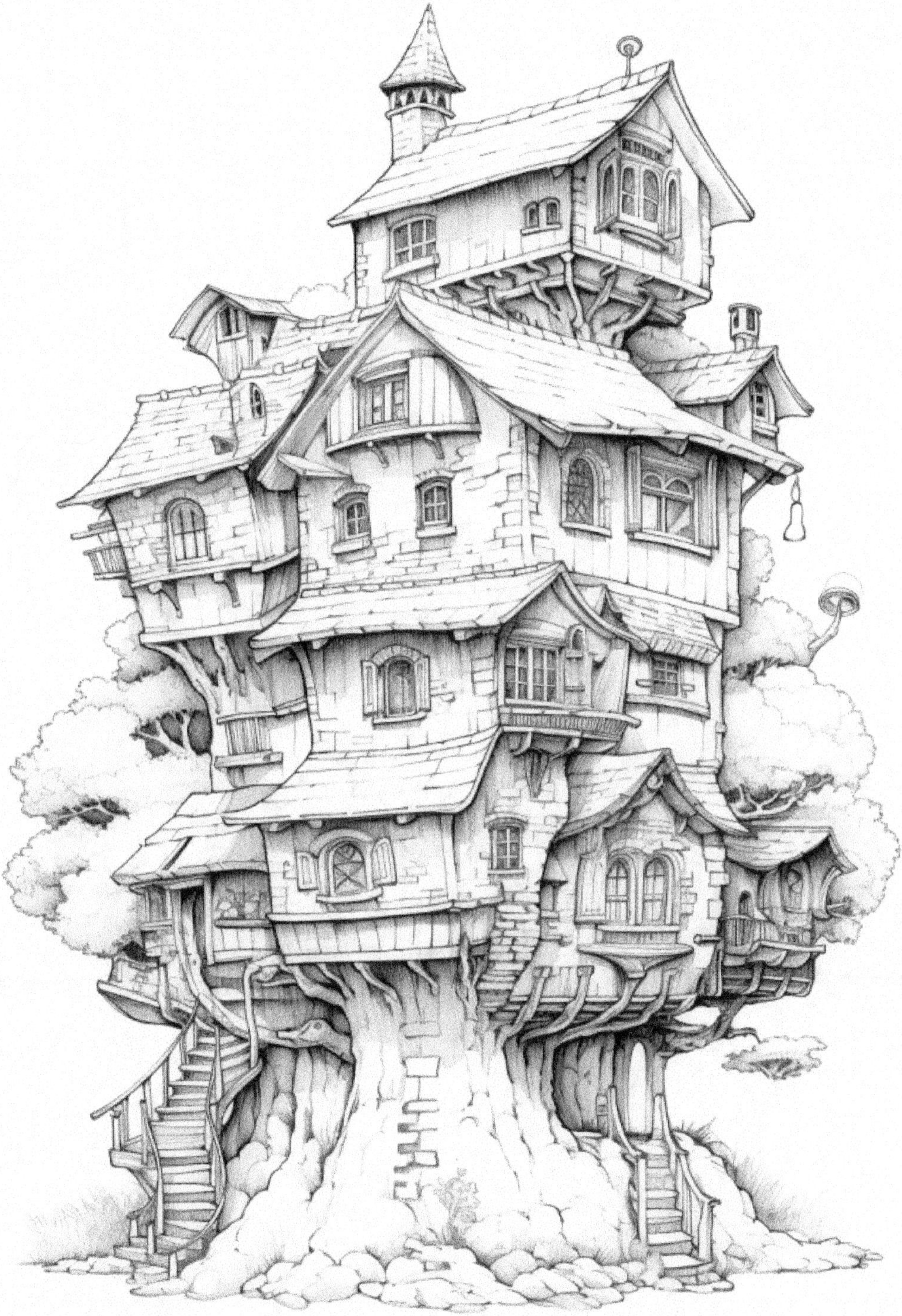

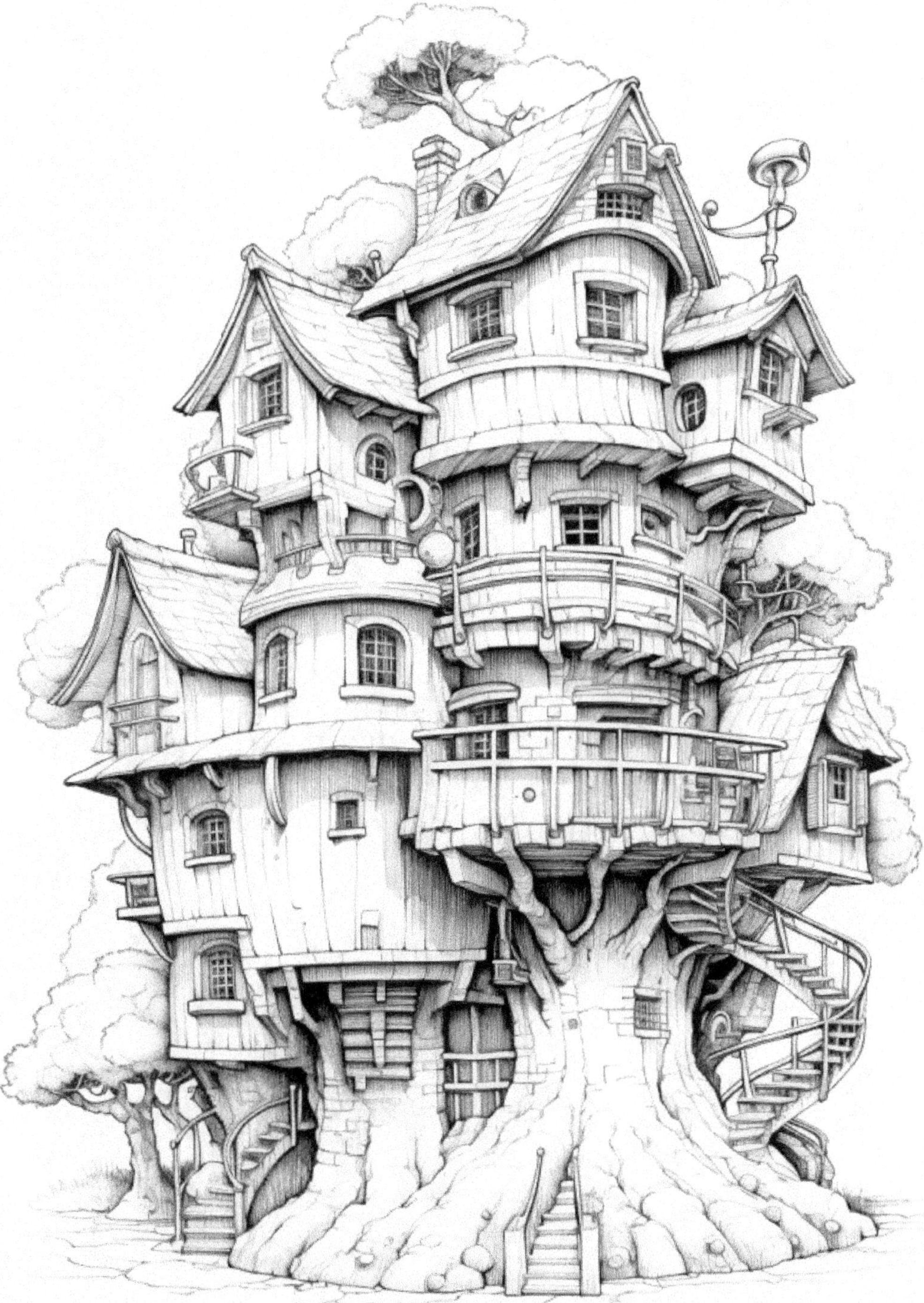

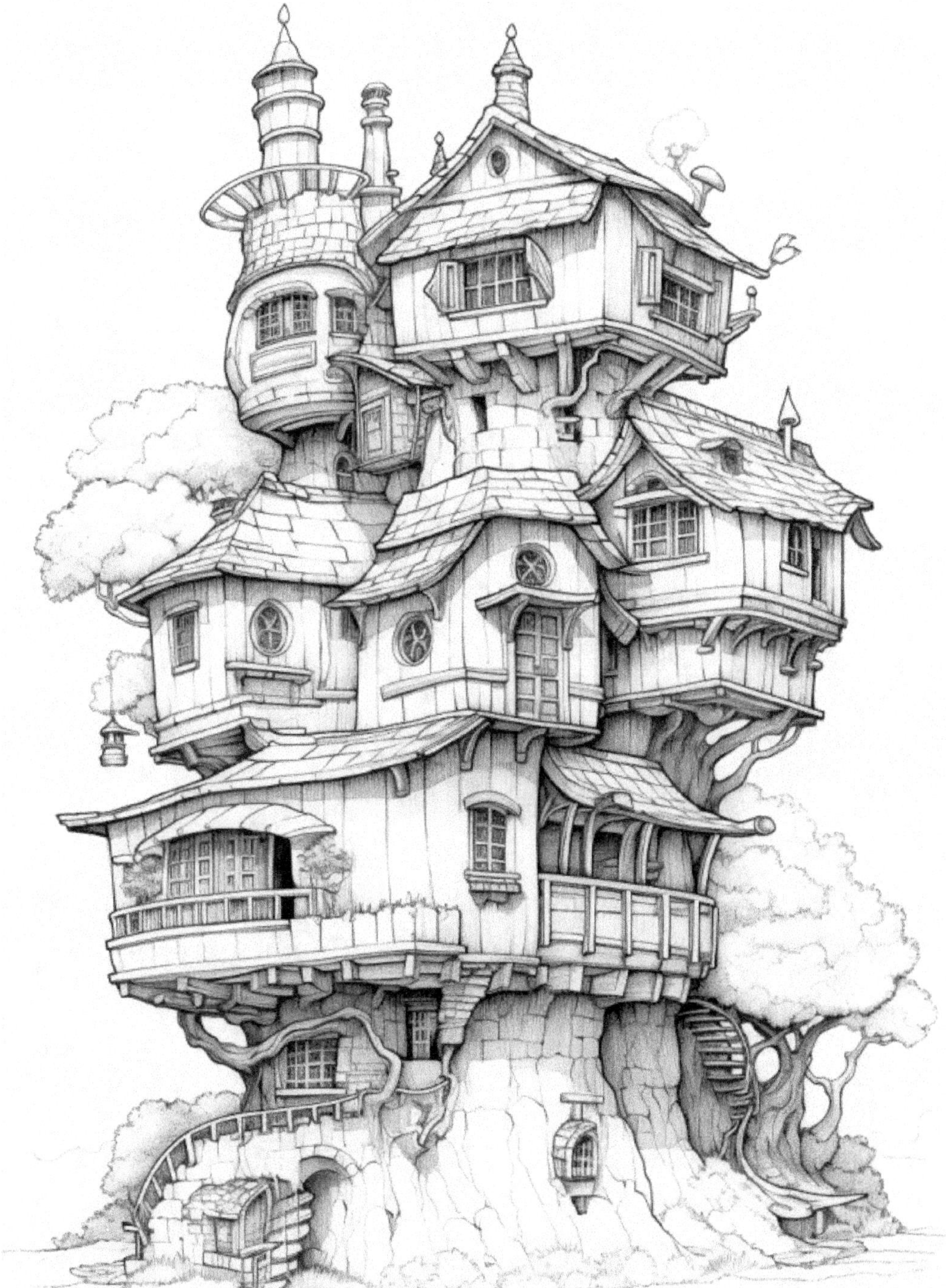

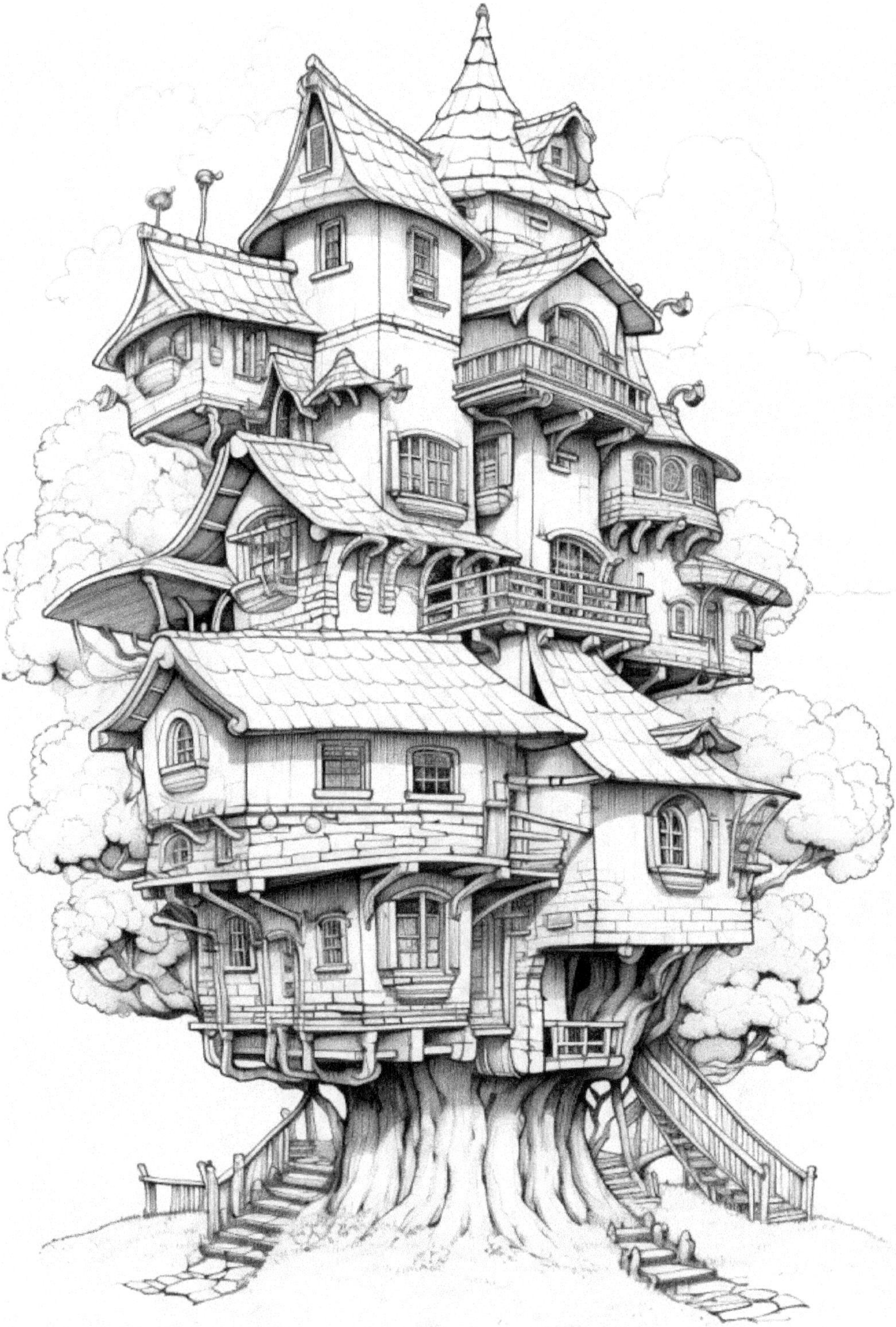

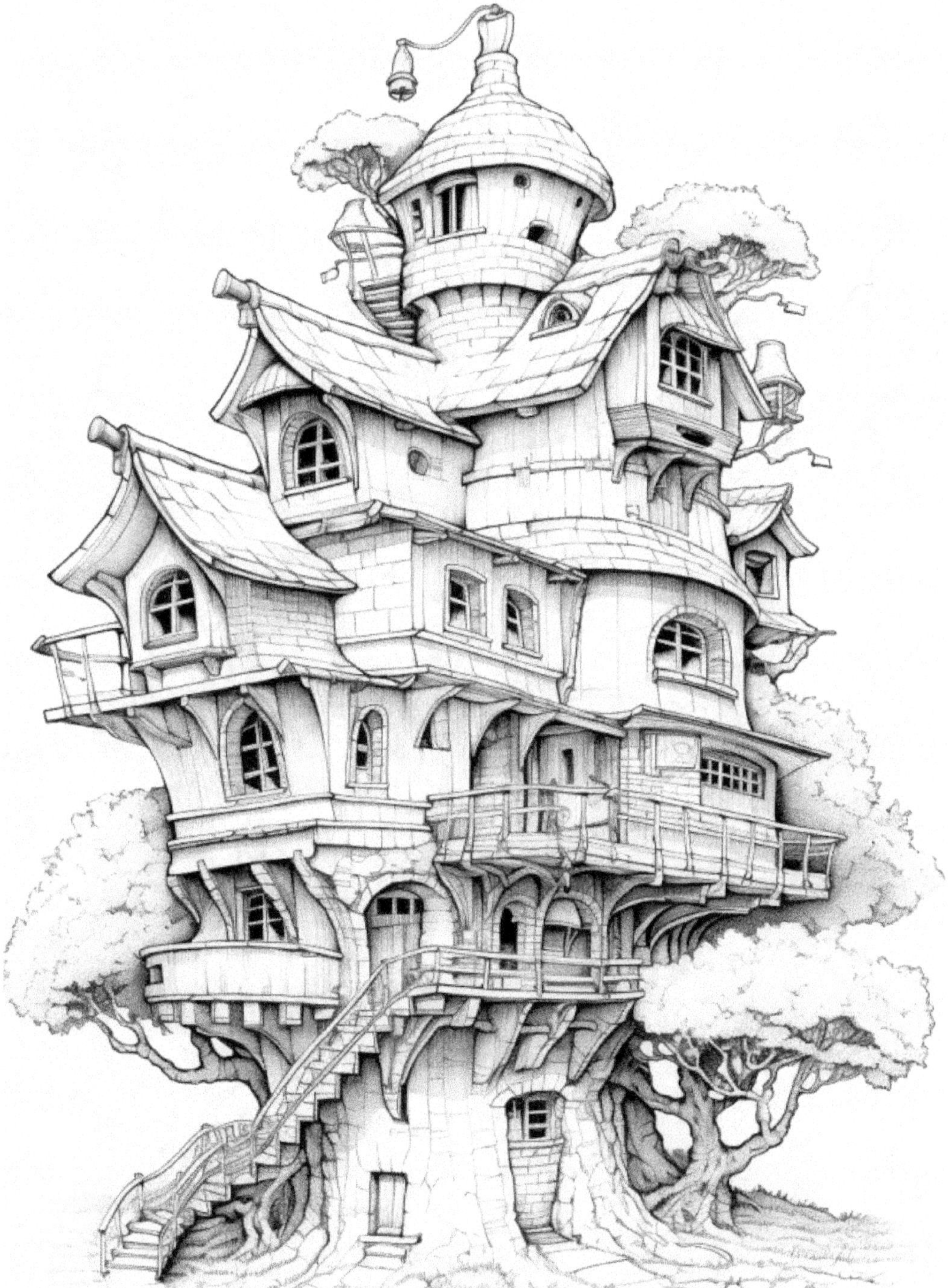

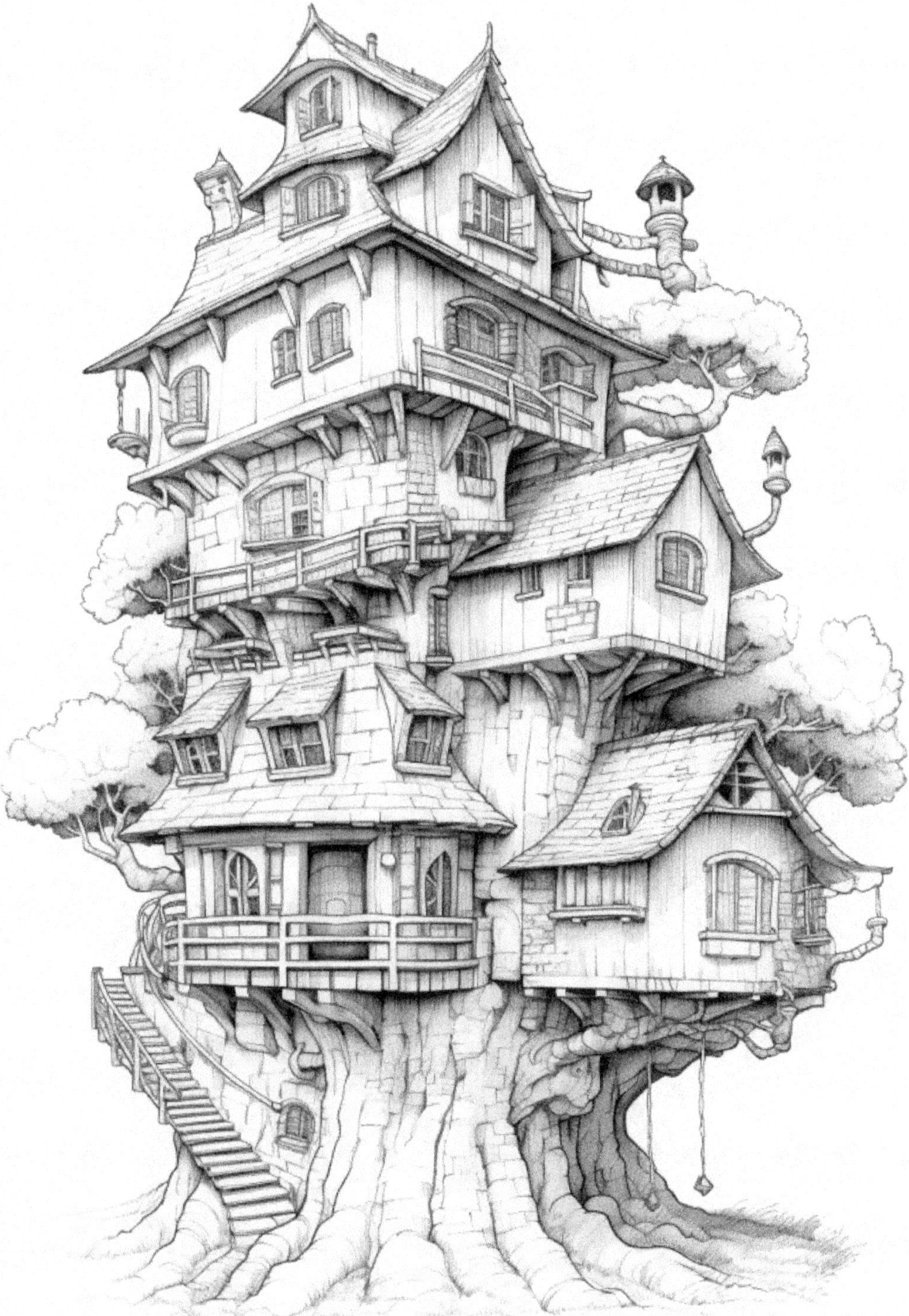

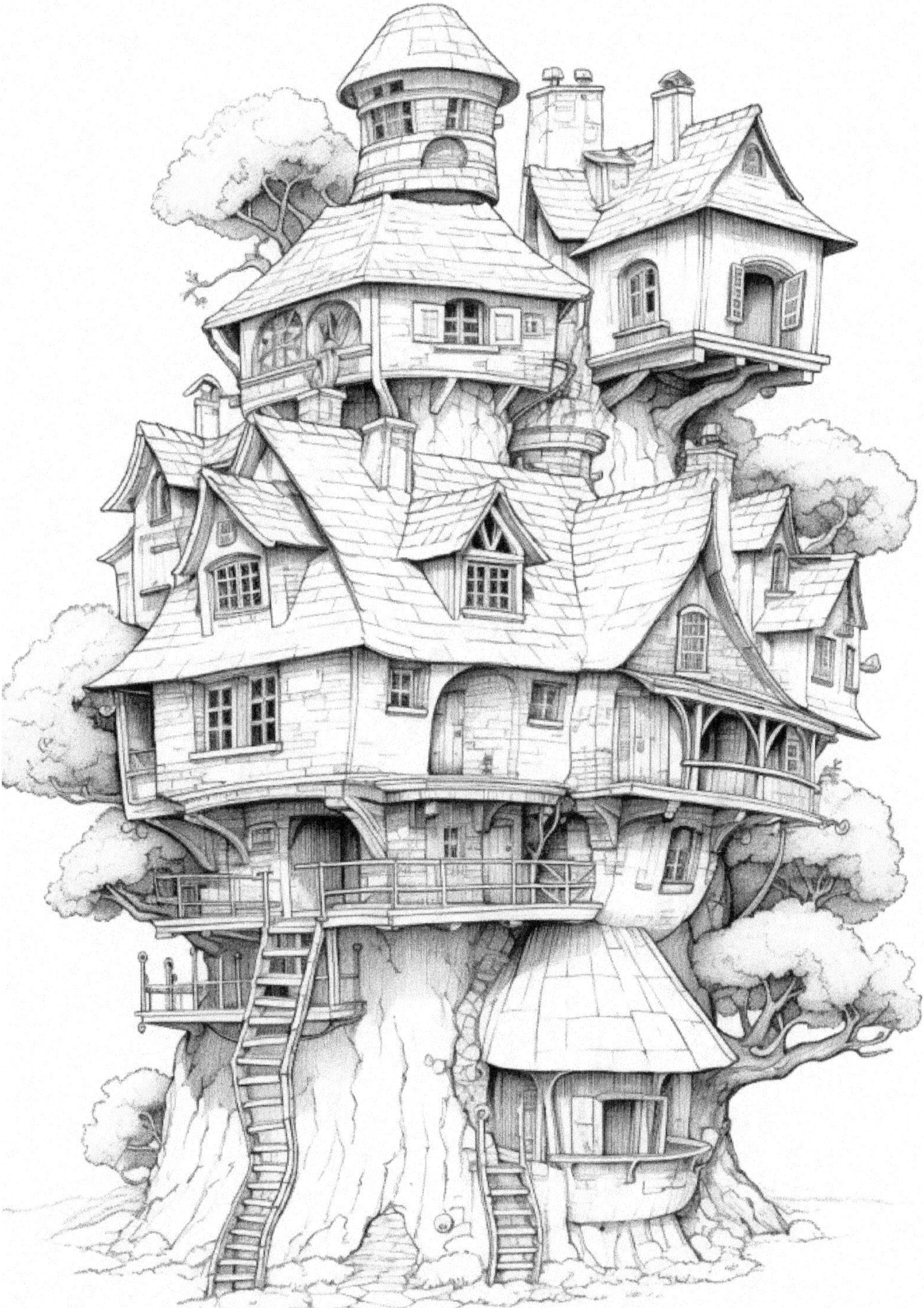

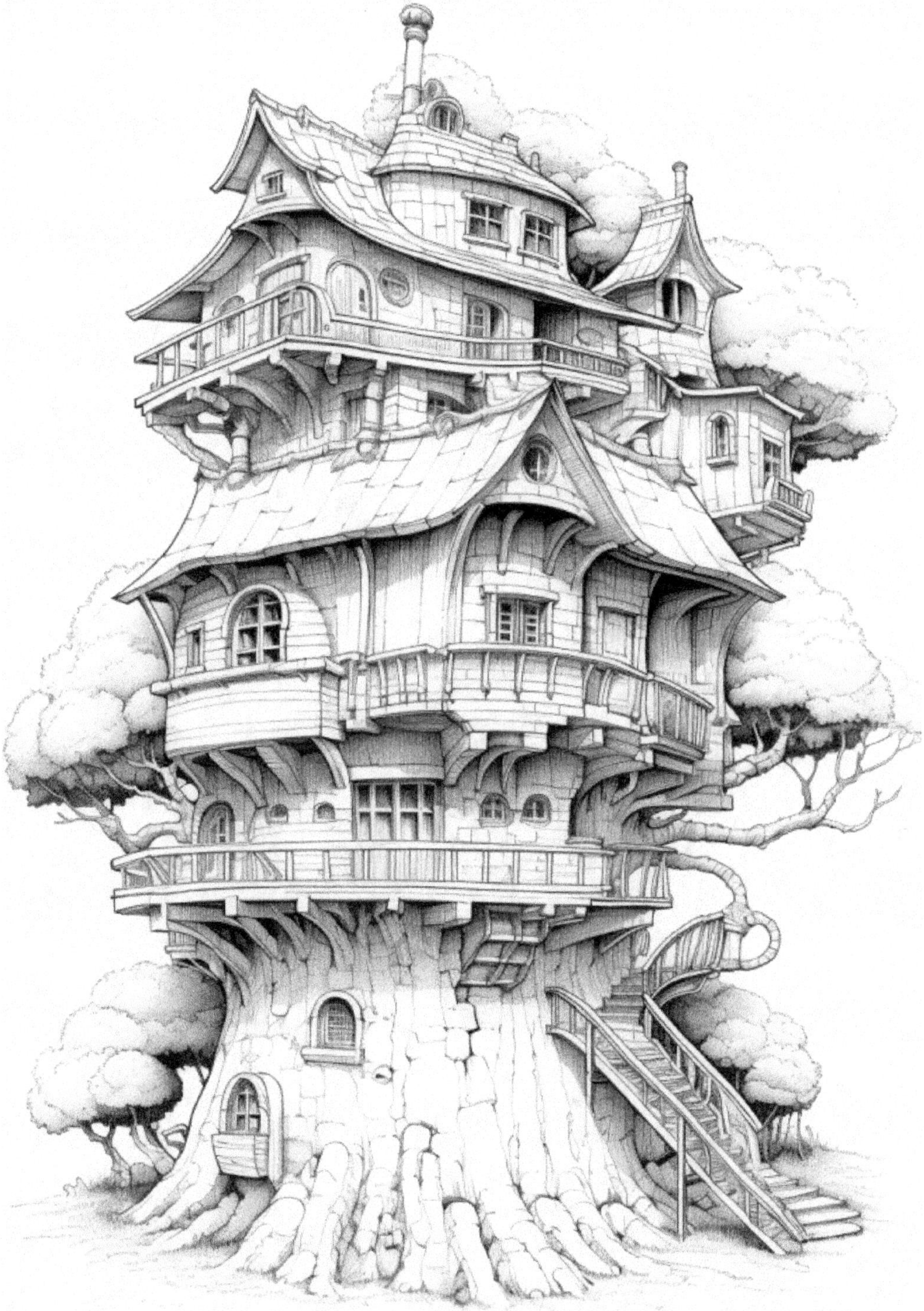

www.ingramcontent.com/pod-product-compliance
Lightning Source LLC
Chambersburg PA
CBHW062237290526
45794CB00006B/2322
* 9 7 9 8 8 5 6 3 9 5 8 4 5 *